Business and the Culture
of Ethics

Business and the Culture of Ethics

Quentin Langley

BEP

BUSINESS EXPERT PRESS

Leader in applied, concise business books

Business and the Culture of Ethics

Copyright © Business Expert Press, LLC, 2020.

Cover image licensed by Ingram Image, StockPhotoSecrets.com

Cover and interior design by Exeter Premedia Services Private Ltd., Chennai, India

First published in 2020 by
Business Expert Press, LLC
222 East 46th Street, New York, NY 10017
www.businessexpertpress.com

ISBN-13: 978-1-95253-822-3 (paperback)
ISBN-13: 978-1-95253-823-0 (e-book)

Business Expert Press Business Ethics and Corporate Citizenship Collection

Collection ISSN: 2333-8806 (print)
Collection ISSN: 2333-8814 (electronic)

First edition: 2020

10 9 8 7 6 5 4 3 2 1

Printed in the United States of America.

Endorsements

"Most books on ethics seem to be written by philosophers and are often very theoretical. This is the book I've been waiting for: a concise, very concrete guide for my students at HEC Montreal business school. Built around scenarios, replete with case studies and containing class and individual exercises, this is an ideal book for the people who will face real ethical decisions in the market place. Quentin Langley has done an outstanding job."—**Germain Belzile, Director of Research, Montreal Economic Institute**

"Can a book examining business ethics in our current - very current - society be more timely - that is, a book rich in case histories from today's headlines, and headlines likely tomorrow, with "players" such as the "princes of the digital age"? I think not. In Business and the Culture of Ethics Quentin Langley delivers a thoughtful and well-informed analysis on front-page, and enduring, subjects ranging from corruption and corporate social responsibility (my favorite) to media ethics and government ethics. This is a book with legs and longevity. I recommend it for teaching business ethics or in business training."—**John Paluszek, Executive Editor, Business in Society**

This book is dedicated to the memory of Malcolm Langley (1920–2017), my father. He did not need Kant or Bentham to tell him what was right or wrong. Having left school at 16, he was largely self-educated, though very well-read. He dedicated his career as a local government auditor to fighting corruption and rose to be the Inspector of Audit for all of England and Wales. His unwavering belief in integrity has been a guiding light in my career and the process of writing this book.

Abstract

Ethics are not the same as morals. They are contextual and apply to specific relationships. This work explores business ethics as applied in a modern context including data management, corporate social responsibility, media ethics and government ethics. Drawing on the work of philosophers, the work is nonetheless contemporary and practical.

Keywords

Ethics; morals; regulation; CSR; accountability; harassment; discrimination; inclusion; animal welfare; environment; compliance; safety; media; government

Contents

How to Use This Book

This book is set out such that it can be used for teaching business ethics in either a university setting or as part of business training.

There are 12 chapters, each covering a distinct teaching unit. General principles of ethics, such as those of Kant and Bentham, are linked to contemporary case studies.

The 12 chapters cover key issues for people with a general interest in business ethics—for example, business majors. In a work setting, more relevant and specific case studies can easily be developed.

For majors in specific business disciplines—finance, marketing, HR, and so on—a deeper dive is going to be necessary in particular areas. Professional societies and institutes provide codes of ethics and case studies that can inform such additional classes.

The chapters contain the following units:

Discussions: Scenarios and questions for in class discussion.
Case studies: Descriptions of real events that illustrate points.
Practical Exercises: Tasks for in or out of class work.
Academic Exercises: For completion out of class.

CHAPTER 1

What Are Ethics?

So, what are ethics, and why should businesses have them?

In ordinary parlance, *ethics* and *morals* are used almost interchangeably. It will be one of the guiding principles of this book that they are, at least in a professional context, slightly different. Morals are absolute guiding principles, whereas ethics are more contextual.

What if you were to tell someone you had committed a murder? What would that person do with the information?

Well, a police officer would probably arrest you. A priest would urge you to repent. A psychotherapist would ask you how it made you feel.

And, a lawyer? Well, that depends if she is *your* lawyer or a prosecutor.

One could argue that the moral response is the same in each case, but the *ethical* response is contextual. We require professionals to follow a particular set of ethics because that is what enables them to do their jobs. People can talk freely to their lawyers or their priest because they know the information is confidential.

Some degree of predictability is valuable to us. We need to understand the rules and the incentives under which people are operating. If a sales representative tells you that the color really suits you and that your butt does not look big in that, you understand that the information is not necessarily reliable, but technical information about the performance of a car or the proper care of a garment *is* supposed to be literally true.

Ethics and morals, as well as incentives, are supposed to guide our decisions.

The Basic Trolley Problem

You are walking by the railway track. You see a train approaching that will kill five people working on the track. You cannot warn them or stop the train. There is only one thing you can do to save them: use the switch to divert the trolley onto another track, where it will kill only one person.

Do you use the switch?

There are all sorts of variations we can introduce. What if the one person is your mother? What if the one person is a child and the five are all in their 90s? Would it be easier if, instead of pulling a lever at the trackside, you were miles away and just had to press a button?

So, why should a business not simply lie to you? Why not tell you that your DeLorean is not only a cool-looking car, but it can also travel in time?

Partly because there are consequences for lying. One is that you can sue a business that makes specific and untrue claims about its products or report it for the crime of fraud. Another is that you will be less likely to trust that same business in the future. It is the same with your romantic partners, isn't it? Once you have caught them lying, you are less likely to trust them in the future.

If your purchase is something as expensive as a car, you are more likely to pursue the legal route. For low-value products, this is less likely. But, supermarkets selling household goods may be particularly concerned about repeat business. If you trust them, you might come back on a weekly basis, which is rather less likely at a car showroom.

The businesses you have to watch are those that do not expect to get any repeat business and are also selling low-value products that you might not bother to sue over. We all understand that vendors at flea markets are not as accountable as Wal-Mart or Toyota.

Large Man on a Bridge

You are crossing a bridge over the railway. The train is approaching a group of five people on the track. You cannot warn the people or pull the lever, but you can stop the train by pushing a sufficiently heavy

---

object into its path. You are not heavy enough to leap into the train's path yourself, but fortunately, there is a very large man crossing the bridge at the same time.

All you have to do is push him off the bridge into the path of the train.

But, of course, we have already talked about this. All of you who said they would kill one person to save five will be perfectly willing to push the man off the bridge.

Won't you?

To appreciate fully the ethics of a business, it is worth exploring why businesses even exist. Why do we have companies? Why cannot people simply cooperate with an extended series of contracts?

In the ancient world, businesses were all sole traders or partnerships. There were no outside investors and no insurance. So, who was responsible for a ship if it sank at the sea? The captain was personally liable for the loss of the ship and its cargo. That is why, captains went down with the ship. They could not afford to go home.

The joint stock company, with external investors, came centuries later. Like insurance, it was invented as a way of financing shipping. It is at least arguable that these financial innovations were as important as the printing press in kicking off the renaissance. Those voyages of discovery and trade would not have happened if no one had financed them.

The leadership of a company has a responsibility to make decisions in the interests of the owners.

But, what about the other publics, or stakeholders, on whom the business depends? Would it be better if the management made decisions in the interests of the workers? Or the customers?

Ultimately, all of these people have to get something out of their dealings with the company. The investors are paid for their investment, and workers for their work. Customers get the product, or service, and need to pay enough to reward both workers and investors. That is why, Adam Smith, the founder of the study of economics, talked about an *invisible hand*[1] guiding people to do something that was no part of their intention. Owners want to attract customers and they want to attract staff.

A business can be set up by its employees. It can be owned by them and only pay investors in interest, not profits. But, there are problems with that model, and it does not suit everybody. If you pay interest to the bank not dividends to shareholders, then that has to be paid even when the business is trading poorly. And, if the business fails, then workers lose their jobs *and* their savings, which puts them in a worse situation than if they were simply employees.

Transplant

You are a doctor. You have five patients waiting for organ transplants. It is urgent.

Fortunately, a perfectly healthy patient comes in for a checkup and is compatible with all the five.

So, you just kill him, whip out his organs, and save the other five, right? Kill one to save five.

If you pulled the lever in the first scenario and said no to the doctor killing a patient, why is this different?

If your answer is "because you are a doctor," then we are getting back to that distinction between morals and ethics.

Doctors are governed by a specific code of ethics. We go to our doctors expecting them to treat us in *our* best interests, not to eye us up for any useful organs we might have.

The cost, if doctors behaved like this, would not just be that one person died. It would be that everyone would stop trusting doctors. We would never go in for checkups. We would only go in when we were seriously ill. There would be no early diagnoses. People would die, who might otherwise have been saved.

Most jurisdictions have a concept of corporate personhood. A company is a separate legal entity from the people who own it and the people who

---

[1] Smith, A. 1759. *The Theory of Moral Sentiments*. London, Andrew Millar and Edinburgh, Alexander Kincaid and J Bell.

work for it. This means, for example, that a company can enter into a contract, it can be made subject to the law, and it can be taxed.

In the United States, this concept has recently come in for some criticism. In part, this stems from the legal case *Citizens United v FEC*.[2] In this case, the Supreme Court found that laws preventing the campaign group, Citizens United, from criticizing Hillary Clinton during an election campaign were a breach of the First Amendment guarantees of freedom of speech.

U.S. Senator Bernie Sanders (I, VT) has suggested a constitutional amendment to establish that the rights set out in the Bill of Rights apply to natural persons only,[3] not to corporate persons. Of course, when people think of the free speech rights of corporations, they think of companies such as Wal-Mart or McDonald's and may not be very worried about their freedom of speech. But, Greenpeace is a corporation too. So are labor unions. So, for that matter, are political parties.

If they are not covered by the First Amendment, then it be would lawful for Congress, or a state, to ban Greenpeace from campaigning on climate change or labor unions from advocating a strike.

That may not be what Senator Sanders intended. The actual wording of the proposed amendment is conflicted on the matter, saying that constitutional rights are for *natural persons only*, but also that they do not extend to *for-profit corporations*, leaving the status of not-for-profit corporations—such as Citizens United—vague.

Corporate persons are not exactly the same as natural persons either. They are accountable to the law, but the worst the law can do to them is fine them. A corporation cannot be sent to prison, though, in extreme cases, its officers can.

How, then does a corporation make decisions? What are its priorities?

*In a free-enterprise, private-property system, a corporate executive is
an employee of the owners of the business. He has direct responsibility to his employers. That responsibility is to conduct the business*

---

[2] https://supremecourt.gov/opinions/09pdf/08-205.pdf

[3] https://sanders.senate.gov/imo/media/doc/Saving-American-Democracy.pdf (accessed September 28, 2019).

in accordance with their desires, which generally will be to make as much money as possible while conforming to the basic rules of the society, both those embodied in law and those embodied in ethical custom. Of course, in some cases his employers may have a different objective. A group of persons might establish a corporation for an eleemosynary purpose—for example, a hospital or a school. The manager of such a corporation will not have money profit as his objectives but the rendering of certain services.

Milton Friedman, The Social Responsibility of Business is to Increase its Profits,The New York Times Times, September 13, 1970 (Magazine), at 32, 33.

Friedman was a Nobel Prize-winning economist and generally regarded as the modern apostle of free market capitalism. His views have been criticized by some ethicists and business theorists, as will be explored in Chapter 5, Corporate Social Responsibility.

For the moment, it is worth noting a couple of things in what he says here.

1. While many people assume the purpose of a corporation is *always* to make money, that is simply not true. *Some* corporations are established with that goal but, as we have seen, charities, campaign groups, and political parties are all corporations too.
2. Friedman also talks about *conforming to the basic rules of the society.* He talks about both law and *ethical custom.* There are direct consequences for breaking the law. Businesses can be prosecuted in criminal law or sued for breaches of civil law, but what are the consequence for breaking ethical custom?

Of course, these same points apply to natural persons just as much as to corporate persons. Many people will seek to maximize their own welfare by, for example, seeking to make as much money as they are able. But others will not. Natural persons, too, can be prosecuted or sued for breaches of the law, but not for ethical lapses. So, why should anyone, corporate or natural, ever comply with *ethical custom*?

We have already discussed some examples. The law, in most jurisdictions, does not require you to pull the lever to save people nor does it ban you from doing so. Your decision to act, or not act, in any of those discussion scenarios is based on your own ethical framework.

There is no doubt that people sometimes lie. Profiles on Tinder have been known to contain exaggerations or even outright fabrications. But, people do not lie all of the time. They do not even lie every time there might be an advantage in doing so.

And, lying is merely a singular example. Most people never steal, murder, or rape either. But, lying is particularly useful example because it is something that everyone has done at some time, but which most people do not do most of the time.

Why not?

Some people attribute their morality to their religion, others to an innate sense that flows from empathy. We do not rape or steal because we know we would not like to be raped or to have our stuff stolen.

But, with basic ethical rules, this moral sense is underscored by a practical factor.

Yes, you could claim to be six inches taller than you really are on your Tinder profile. But, what advantage derives from this? Maybe you get more first dates, but you cannot maintain the deception past the first moment of meeting. Your chance for a second date is reduced, rather than increased.

Other deceptions can be maintained much longer. You could lie about your income, for example, and it is certainly possible that you could maintain that lie long enough to get what you were hoping for.

In the old quote often (without evidence) attributed to Abraham Lincoln:

You can fool all of the people some of the time, you can fool some of the people all of the time, but you cannot fool all the people all of the time.

People use the game theory to analyze behavior in the market. But, the real market is not a game. Many of the scenarios in the game theory assume a one-off interaction and no communication between the parties.

That is not realistic. Often, in the real market, a business will want to promote repeat business. And, customers do communicate with each other. There are ratings systems promoted by Yelp, Amazon, the Better Business Bureau, and many others.

But, customers are not the only people on whom a business depends. Businesses also need to attract investors, staff, business partners, and many others. If a business is widely seen as operating unethically, this may be a challenge.

To compete, you may need to attract high-quality staff. That is not just a matter of paying more money. People report that they seek more than that in a job. They consider things such as job satisfaction and the ethics of the organization. Of course, people also say they think that everyone else considers only the money. So, either people are wrong in estimating how other people behave or they are lying about their own behavior.

Certainly, when Shell faced a couple of major crises in the 1990s—surrounding the disposal of a used oil storage platform in the North Sea and the company's relationship with the then military dictatorship in Nigeria—it found it was meeting resistance at graduate recruitment fairs. Major engineering companies are focused on the long term. If the company cannot attract the best graduates, then who will run the business in 40 years' time?

So, are these pragmatic considerations the only ones that matter?

Thinkers have long been divided on this question. Immanuel Kant believed that people are governed by a *categorical imperative* to do the right thing.[4]

Let us imagine that a Terminator cyborg from the future has asked you if you know where Sarah Connor is. You know that if you tell the Terminator where she is, the Terminator will kill her, dooming not just her, but future generations as well.

Do you lie and send the Terminator in the wrong direction? Or, how about SS troops looking for a Jewish family?

When is it okay to lie?

Kant would argue never.

---

[4] Kant, I. 1785. *Groundwork of the Metaphysic of Morals*. Riga: Johann Friedrich Hartknoch.

So, why did Kant think lying was always bad? Because if everyone lied all of the time, the results would be bad. Therefore, we can tell that lying is bad, and if it is bad, then it is always bad, and there is no room for individual judgments. That is the categorical imperative. Lying is in a category of wrong things, and anything in that category is wrong.

Kant believed every person is responsible for his or her own actions. If those SS troops kill the Jewish family, that is not your fault. It is entirely on the consciences of the troops involved.

Not only that, it is possible that your well-intentioned intervention will make the situation worse. Let us suppose you send the SS to the house next door, but in a stroke of bad luck, that is the exact direction the Jewish family is fleeing. In this instance, they are killed precisely *because* of your intervention. Your lie caused them to be killed. Kant would argue that, in this case, you are at fault, whereas by telling the truth, you can never be at fault.

Let us go back to that basic trolley problem. Did you choose to pull the lever? Not everyone does. Some people argue that pulling the lever is *playing god*. *Letting* five people die is not as bad as *actively killing* one person.

That is similar to Kant's reasoning. If you tell the truth, all the responsibility for the death of the Jewish family falls on the SS. But, if they are killed because of your lie, then you bear a share of the guilt as well.

Not all thinkers have agreed with Kant, of course.

Jeremy Bentham was one of the founders of the utilitarian school of thought. He believed in pursuing the greatest happiness for the greatest number of people.[5] He would definitely have pulled the lever, lied to the SS and to the Terminator as well.

Sure, that might have gone wrong. Maybe the Terminator would kill Sarah Connor *because* of Bentham's lie. He could not know for sure what she was planning to do next. But, as long as he acted in good faith, on his best estimate of the likely consequences, then he could know that he had done the right thing.

---

[5] Bentham, J. 1776. *A Fragment on Government.* London: Printed for T. Payne ... P. Elmsly ... and E. Brook.

Utilitarianism is a *consequentialist* school of thought. You should plot out the likely consequences of your actions and decide whether they are good or bad. Nothing—lying, killing people, rape—is good or bad of itself. It is the *consequences* of the action that determine whether it is good or bad. Kant's reasoning, by contrast, is a form of deontology, based on the notion that the act itself is either right or wrong.

The Ticking Bomb

You know there is a ticking bomb somewhere in the city. Worse, it is a dirty bomb. Setting it off will release radioactive waste, toxic chemical agents, and a mutated form of smallpox into the atmosphere.

Millions will die.

You have captured the terrorist who planted the bomb, which you think is due to go off in the next 20 minutes. There will not be time for an evacuation.

You have absolutely no qualms about torturing the terrorist to get the information. Why would you? Millions will die if you cannot defuse the bomb in time. But, he has been trained for this. All your instincts tell you that he will not break under torture. You would just be wasting precious time.

Fortunately, there is another solution. The terrorist deeply, deeply, loves his daughter.

All you have to do is torture *her* until he breaks. Then, you can save millions of people.

So, torturing his daughter is just fine, right? Did I mention that she's seven years old and knows nothing of her dad's role as a terrorist?

There is no doubt that Kant's deontology can put you in some difficult situations, such as telling the SS that the Frank family is in the attic. But, Bentham's consequentialist reasoning can lead to you torturing seven-year-old girls.

How should a business deal with ethical issues? Are there some categorical lines that it should never cross, whatever the consequences, or should it be guided by its best, good faith, estimate as to the consequences?

Adam Smith argued that the ethics of a business were unreliable and irrelevant.

It is not that people running businesses were not ethical people. It is simply that, as a consumer, you could not know about the personal ethics of the officers of a company. What you could know is what is in their best interests and predict their behavior on that basis.

In his foundational text *Wealth of Nations*,[6] he argued:

> *It is not from the benevolence of the butcher, the brewer, or the baker that we expect our dinner, but from their regard to their own interest.*

None of these shopkeepers might care about your dinner in any way. But, supplying you with the means to eat is the means by which they eat.

So, Smith was arguing that pursuing self-interest can produce results that benefit both you and others. Bentham would (and did) approve.

This division between deontological and consequentialist schools of thought is one of the most fundamental divisions in ethical thought. Another such division is between ethical or moral relativism and universalism. We will see this one play out particularly in Chapter 3 (Corruption). Is there one set of rules that is right for all places and times or do notions of *good* and *bad* change from one place or time to another?

The Catholic church has been particularly critical of moral relativism. It attributes what it sees as the moral degeneracy of Europe and other western societies to the abandonment of traditional notions of right and wrong. In particular, in Catholic theology, the conscious breaking of the link between sexual intercourse and procreation is wrong.

In Catholicism—and in religious traditions generally—morality comes from god. It is, therefore, unchanging. The invention of the contraceptive pill and growing social acceptance of gay relationships do not change what god has ordained.

But, if we are to argue that morality never changes, then we must ask from what does it never change. Many Christian traditions now accept the ordination of women as priests and that priests—whether male or female—may be married. The Catholic church does not. But, it has not

---

[6] Smith, A. 1776. *An Inquiry into the Nature and Causes of the Wealth of Nations.* London: William Strahan.

always insisted on unmarried celibacy for its priests. This rule was instituted by Pope Gregory VII in the 12th century.

The history of Christian churches with regard to slavery is long and complex. Some Christians have argued that there is a distinction between *just* and *unjust* slavery, but this has sometimes been vague. Some have argued that it is impermissible to hold baptized Christians as slaves, and others have taken the much more restrictive view—also specified in the 13th Amendment to the U.S. Constitution—that slavery is only acceptable as punishment for convicted criminals.

So, even the view that universal rules are divine allows for some change: presumably in human interpretation of divine rules rather than in the rules themselves. If there was a time when human morality was correct, when was it? Presumably, some time between the abolition of slavery and the invention of the contraceptive pill.

But, moral relativism is not without its own complications.

While there are certainly moral issues with seeking to impose one society's set of rules on another, is that not what the Allies did in Germany in 1945? If one set of rules is as good as another, then perhaps, you *should* have betrayed the Frank family to the SS. That was the law in that particular time and place.

So, we have explored the difference between general morality and professional ethics. The doctor does not kill one patient for the benefit of five others, though the operator of the rail network might.

We have looked at the reasons why businesses behave ethically, or unethically.

And, we have looked at the ideas of some famous philosophers—Kant and Bentham—on how to tell if an action is good or bad.

In the coming chapters, we will look at some specific examples. How and why should businesses care about the environment? About diversity and harassment in the workforce? About animal welfare?

Practical Exercise

Debate the motion: **This house believes that a public relations professional should never lie for a client.**

Note: it says lie *for* a client, not lie *to* a client.

Think about issues of trust here. Remember the boy who cried *wolf*. If you lie for the client, you undermine your client's trust. And your own. Will anyone ever give you a job in the future if people are not likely to believe you?

But, that word *never* is pretty strong. Does my butt look big in this?

And, what about your client's privacy? What if your client is an NBA player and does not want the other players to know that he is gay? Would you lie to a journalist to keep that story out of the media?

British publicist, Max Clifford, says he lied to preserve the privacy of a gay soccer player in the English Premier League. He did it knowing that only one player in the EPL had ever come out as gay, and he committed suicide.

And, maybe your athlete client is not playing in Britain or America. Maybe, it is Russia or Saudi Arabia.

Academic Exercise

Write an academic reflection on what you have learned preparing for and participating in the debate.

Use some of the formal academic reflection models such as those of Bereiter and Scardamalia (1993), Kolb (1984), or Chinn and Kramer (1995). (There are many more.)

For freshmen students, I specify using at least one of the reflection models. For more experienced students, I specify using at least two models and then reaching an integrated conclusion, which draws on the learning from both reflections.

Resources

Three Minute Philosophy, Kant: https://youtu.be/xwOCmJevigw
PR Week debate: Max Clifford versus George Pitcher: https://prweek.com/article/635672/emprweek-em-ethics-debate-truth-hurts
Three Minute Philosophy, Utilitarianism: https://youtu.be/wS9bey162PU
Ethics Redefined, Moral Relativism: https://youtu.be/5RU7M6JSVtk
Steven Pinker Redefines Moral Relativism: https://youtu.be/ASL4cwU_3tc

CHAPTER 2

The Moral Palette

What are the foundations of morality? This is not a debate about whether morality is an innate evolutionary response or a gift from a deity. This is about a possibly more fundamental question. What sort of question is a moral question?

Is it, for example, about harming people? Is it a matter of fairness? If so, what constitutes *fair*? It was once very widely accepted that some sexual practices, even when consensual, are immoral. There is no such consensus on that in western countries today, though it remains a widely held view.

Graham, Haidt, et al. set out a moral foundations theory[1] in which they defined five dimensions to morality and linked them to evolutionary psychology. They found evidence for these five foundations in human societies across the globe and in other primate societies. This research was later popularized by Jonathan Haidt in his book, *The Righteous Mind*.[2]

The original foundations are:

- The care/harm foundation
- The fairness/cheating foundation
- The loyalty/betrayal foundation
- The authority/subversion foundation
- The sanctity/degradation foundation

[1] Graham, J.; Haidt, J.; Koleva, S.; Motyl, M.; Iyer, R.; Wojcik, S.; Ditto, P.H. Ditto. 2013. "Moral Foundations Theory: The Pragmatic Validity of Moral Pluralism (PDF)." *Advances in Experimental Social Psychology* 47, pp. 55–130.

[2] Haidt, J. 2012. *The Righteous Mind: Why Good People Are Divided by Politics and Religion*. New York, NY: Pantheon Books.

Under challenge from conservatives and libertarians, Haidt subsequently added:

- The liberty/oppression foundation

Haidt set out how liberals and conservatives—we are, here, following American terminology, where *liberal* denotes the political left—focus heavily on the first two foundations, whereas conservatives tend to draw on all five or six.

The first foundation is obvious. If something harms someone, then it is immoral. Consensual sexual acts rarely harm someone. But, what if they do? In Britain, the House of Lords (then the supreme court for England and Wales) judgment in *R v, Brown*[3] (sometimes referred to as *the spanner case*) was that consent was not a valid defense in cases of actual bodily harm. This referred the prosecution of 16 gay and bisexual men involved in sadomasochism. There is no need to go into the details, but some of the individuals incurred real, but consensual, injuries.

But, if consent is not a defense in the case of actual bodily harm, does that mean that boxing is illegal in England and Wales? Apparently not though, very obviously, what boxers do to each other would be illegal in the absence of consent. Norway, Cuba, and North Korea have all banned boxing on the grounds that it harms people.

Sexually motivated sadomasochism seems to offend as much against *sanctity* as against the care or harm foundation.

While both liberals and conservatives see fairness as an important element of morality, they somewhat differ on their notion of what is fair. The far-left notion of fairness was set out by Karl Marx in his *Critique of the Gotha Programme*:[4] "From each according to his ability, to each according to his needs." The conservative notion of fairness might be best related to the Buddhist doctrine of *karma*: you reap what you sow. You may not get what you need, but you should get what you deserve. This

---

[3] http://cirp.org/library/legal/UKlaw/rvbrown1993/
[4] Marx, K., Engels, F., Lenin, V.I., Czobel, E. 1970. *Critique of the Gotha Programme*. New York, NY: International Publishers.

is why arguments about inequality seem to get nowhere. Obviously, no one *needs* to be as rich as Jeff Bezos, but that is not enough to convince conservatives that Bezos does not *deserve* his wealth. That is more focused on the question of whether it was justly acquired.

Loyalty refers to in-group loyalty such as to family, nation, and so on. This is one the foundations that features much less for liberals than for conservatives.

This is also true of authority and respect for tradition. As with loyalty, this is not to say that this is not a feature for liberals at all, just that it is not prioritized as highly as by conservatives. It is common for liberals to argue that while loyalty and respect for tradition may be good things, they are not really connected with morality. Though here the political divide is also about a different locus of trust. The left tends to trust government more than business, whereas the right trusts business more than government. Both are subject to some degree of accountability. Business is subject to the individual accountability that you can boycott a company you do not like. Government is subject to collective accountability. You can vote to change your government, but the government only changes if enough other people agree with you. It is equally true that your boycott is unlikely to change the behavior of a business unless sufficient others join it, but in this case, at least you will have boycotted the business and maintain your own good conscience, even if there is no change on the part of the business.

The fifth point, sanctity, or respect for the sacred, is another point that divides Americans—and probably people in other countries—along political lines. While, across the political spectrum, Americans tend to regard their flag as being *sacred*, this tends to be more strongly felt on the political right. As Haidt has pointed out,[5] while conservatives sacralize sex, try ordering breakfast with a liberal. Liberals sacralize food, with a range of cross-cutting issues, such as organic, Genetically Modified Organisms (GMO), animal welfare, and fair trade.

---

[5] Haidt, J. 2013. "It's Hard to Gross Out a Libertarian: Jonathan Haidt on Sex, Politics, and Disgust. Reason TV." Available on YouTube.

Armin Meiwes—The Rotenburg Cannibal

In 2001, Meiwes placed an ad on a website for people with a fetish for cannibalism. He was seeking a "young well-built man, who wanted to be eaten." Bernd Brandes replied.

They agreed how to proceed. They surgically removed Brandes's penis, fried it, and tried to consume it. The penis was too burned, though, so Meiwes fed it to his dog. Brandes, of course, was bleeding profusely, so Meiwes withdrew to read a *Star Trek* novel. A few hours later he killed Brandes by stabbing him in the throat. He then cut up the body and froze the meat, eating it over several months.

In 2002, Meiwes was convicted of manslaughter.

In 2005, he was retried, and this time convicted of murder.

Explain whether and why you think what Meiwes and Brandes did was wrong.

To many people, it is obvious that the emotion of disgust is closely related to morality. To others, the things are unconnected. You can find a particular sexual or dietary practice disgusting without thinking that it is immoral. Also, many things that are immoral may produce no particular visceral reaction.

Soylent Green—SPOILER

The movie, *Soylent Green*, came out in 1973, so there is probably no ethical problem with including a spoiler here, but it is good to declare it anyway.

The setting is a dystopian future of overpopulation—a popular fear in the 1970s—and mass shortages of everything, including food. There is mass unemployment and poverty. One of the main characters is a senior police officer. When he visits the apartment of a very rich person, he sees soap for the first time. Women are virtual slaves, working as concubines and referred to as *furniture*. (The movie, incidentally, is set in what is, at the time of writing, the very near future: 2022. As prediction it seems to have failed badly.)

Food supplies are controlled by the Soylent Corporation (from *soya* and *lentil* and unconnected with the current products using that name that have been produced by Rosa Foods since 2014). The most popular product line is Soylent Green, although it is often in short supply. It emerges through the police investigations that Soylent Green is actually made from the carcasses of dead humans. The final revelation is Charlton Heston's character yelling "Soylent Green is people."

Of course, Soylent Green is not people. It is simply what happens to their bodies when the people have finished with them.

It is plainly unethical to deceive consumers about the content of the product. This was an issue with the horse meat scandal in the United Kingdom in 2013, where supermarket-ready meals turned out to contain some horse meat—a premium meat product in some countries, but not widely consumed in the UK. But, if the fictional Soylent Corporation had been transparent about its product, would that have been unethical?

Characters in the movie raise the suggestion that consuming human flesh is a *slippery slope:* the next stage will be keeping people as livestock. But, in the context of a food shortage, that makes no sense. The farmed humans would need to be fed. A people farm would consume more food than it produced. Gramnivores, such as sheep and cows (and horses, come to that) consume grass. They can eat vegetable matter, which humans cannot digest, and convert it into food for people. Humans, self-evidently, cannot be used in this way.

Finally, there is the question of freedom and coercion. It goes to the heart of why rape is widely outlawed, and boxing is legal in the vast majority of countries.

It is perfectly clear that many people might think that a person should do something but stop short of wanting people to be forced to do that same thing. An obvious place to start is with matters of good manners. It is a good thing to hold the door open for the person following you. But, few people would argue that this should be the law.

Of course, there are practical constraints here. How far behind you does the person have to be for holding the door to be obligatory? If the person is too far away, might they feel pressured to hurry? Does there come a point when holding the door is rude? If that is the case, and holding the door is compulsory, should there also be a point at which it is banned?

Of course, things that were once considered merely a matter of manners—telling dirty or racially insensitive jokes, for example—can now cross the line into sexual or racial harassment.

Nonetheless, almost everyone agrees that there are some things that are good, but that should not be compulsory, and others that are bad but should not be banned. Coercion is a negative factor. To some libertarians, it is almost the only moral consideration, but almost everyone accepts it has some role in moral decision making.

The Future of Meat

There are now various plant-based fake meats available. While vegeburgers are not new, modern techniques can produce something much closer to meat in terms of texture and flavor.

Some U.S. states have considered laws to prevent the use of the word *meat* or *burger* in products that are entirely plant- or mushroom-based.

There are also methods of producing real meat in laboratories. This product is chemically identical to meat, but with huge quantities synthesized from a tiny number of animal cells. Real meat, made without any animal having to die. No more worrying about the conditions in which the animals are held or the carbon footprint of animal rearing.

Would you eat synthetic meat, produced in a laboratory?

Science fiction author Douglas Adams[6] developed another solution: animals that have been bred with a desire to be eaten and the cognitive skills to come to your table and tell you so. The Ameglion Major Cow will explain that it has been exercising hard so its haunches will be nice and lean for you.

Would you eat an animal that wants to be eaten?

Do you eat animals that *do not* want to be eaten?

Why?

---

[6] Adams, D. 1980, *Restaurant at the End of the Universe*. London, Pan Books.

Many people have argued that insects will be a major source of protein in people's diets in the future. Eating insects may disgust some people, but eating dogs and cats is normal in some cultures, and considered revolting in others.

Should we see a connection between disgust and morality?

Practical Exercise

Choose a controversial statement and prepare arguments for and against the statement. Be prepared to defend a stance on this subject orally in front of the class in an aggressive interview. Which side you take will be determined by the toss of a coin at the beginning of the interview.

Sample Controversial Statements:

Abortion is murder.

It is not ethical to eat meat.

Animal testing should be banned.

Assisted dying should be illegal.

There should be capital punishment for child abuse.

Drug prohibition should end.

Vaccination of children should be compulsory.

Plastic straws should be prohibited.

It is time to repeal laws on incest.

Inequality is *the* most important policy issue.

Iran should be prevented from acquiring nuclear weapons, by force if necessary.

Boxing should be banned.

People convicted of serious crimes should be permanently banned from voting.

It should be illegal to label plant-based products with names that suggest meat, such as *burger* or *Unchicken*.

The age of consent should be raised.

Wearing fur in public should be illegal.

Genetically modified crops should be banned.

We should welcome the concept of *designer babies*.

The minimum wage does more harm than good.

Faith is just an excuse to avoid rational thought.

Academic Exercise

Write an essay exploring the title: **Conservatives generally have a good understanding of liberal morality. They just do not agree. Liberals, by contrast, do not really understand conservatives.**

Look at arguments that tend to support the proposition and arguments that tend to refute it. Reach a reasoned conclusion

---

Resources

Jonathan Haidt, The moral roots of liberals and conservatives, TED: https://youtu.be/8SOQduoLgRw

CHAPTER 3

Corruption

Corruption

Noun

1. the act of corrupting or state of being corrupt
2. moral perversion; depravity
3. perversion of integrity
4. corrupt or dishonest proceedings
5. bribery
6. debasement or alteration, as of language or a text

Dictionary.com

In general, corruption is a form of dishonesty or criminal activity undertaken by a person or organization entrusted with a position of authority, often to acquire illicit benefit. Corruption may include many activities, including bribery and embezzlement, though it may also involve practices that are legal in many countries.

Wikipedia

Corruption is the abuse of entrusted power for private gain. It can be classified as grand, petty, and political, depending on the amounts of money lost and the sector where it occurs.

Transparency International

Do You Pay?

You have just been appointed the general manager of your company's subsidiary in the Middle African Republic. The company builds infrastructure projects such as roads, dams, power stations, and so on.

The Deputy General Manager of the business is a local and explains to you that the Minister of Infrastructure and Development is his brother-in-law. The minister maintains a bank account in Switzerland and expects to be paid a fee before the business can arrange a meeting with him. There is a further fee if you want to be invited to submit a tender for building the new power station. The largest fee, of course, is to ensure that your tender is the one accepted.

You do not really know how to react to this. You are not completely surprised. Transparency International ranks countries by how corrupt they are, and you knew that the Middle African Republic was toward the bottom.

Your first thought is that it is not fair. But, it is not as if any of the other western companies will be competing honestly. That is just how contracts are awarded in some countries. Really, the western companies are the victims here. The minister is extorting money from them.

Or, maybe you are just paying taxes. You hand the money over to the government, just as you do in western countries. It is not your fault that the minister siphons the money away for his own purposes.

So, it is fine to pay the bribe, isn't it?

Well, the law in the United States and in an increasing group of other western countries is that no, it is not ever okay to pay a bribe. This may be legal and, indeed, customary in some countries, but businesses that are registered in the United States or that have securities traded in the United States (e.g., shares quoted on the New York Stock Exchange) are forbidden to engage in such practices. Ever.

The Foreign and Corrupt Practices Act of 1977 outlaws making payments (monetary or otherwise) to officials, candidates, parties, or intermediaries for the purpose of winning or retaining business. It is not limited to government officials. It covers making a similar payment to the CEO of a business.

The United States was well ahead of many other western countries in adopting such legislation. The United Kingdom, for example, adopted similar provisions in the Bribery Act of 2010. It is possible that American corporations lost out on business because rivals from other countries were allowed to pay bribes when American businesses were not.

Certainly, as per our example, it is when engaging in international business that the most challenging situations will arise.

In the United States, if you were to make a direct payment to an official, it would be clearly against the law. Everyone would agree that this was something to be hidden from view. In some countries, such behavior is perfectly normal. There is no agreement that it is wrong or shameful.

But, does that mean that such things do not go on in the United States, or that, when they do, they are necessarily illegal?

Not exactly. There may be disguised ways of making payments that effectively amount to bribes.

Businesses can make large payments to a candidate's election campaign. That is perfectly legal.

While Hillary Clinton was Secretary of State, her husband and daughter were both employed by the Clinton Family Foundation. This is an organization that has done a great deal of good work and has received donations from many individuals and businesses. Doug Band, an official at the foundation and an aide to her husband, occasionally asked the Secretary for favors on behalf of *friends* of the foundation, such as agreeing to meet people.

Ruth Marcus, a liberal, Democratic-supporting, columnist for the *Washington* Post, headlined her column on the subject: *Obliging a donor is not necessarily criminal.* She is right. It is not. There is actual legal precedent to that effect.

Governor Bob McDonnell (R. VA) and his wife were indicted and initially convicted on federal corruption charges for accepting *personal* gifts from a donor. These were not donations to his campaign fund or to a charity employing members of his family. They included such things as a Rolex watch.

But, the Supreme Court unanimously vacated their convictions. The court ruled that the trial court had taken a much too broad a view of the term *official act* by including, for example, setting up meetings. By that standard, not only was Clinton's behavior not criminal, but still would not have been if payments had been made directly to her and not to the charitable foundation that bore her name and employed members of her family.

Senator Bob Menendez (D. NJ) was tried on corruption charges over his advocacy for a campaign donor and friend, a Florida ophthalmologist. The jury, applying the McDonnell standard, was unable to reach a verdict. The Department of Justice decided not to re-file charges, so the matter was dropped. The Senate committee on ethics severely admonished Menendez. Despite a primary challenge, Menendez was nonetheless reelected to the Senate in the same year as the letter of admonishment.

It is not enough to prove bad behavior on the part of an official and financial payments from the other party. Prosecutors now have to prove both a specific *official act* (from a narrowed list of such acts) and a *quid pro quo*. If I pay you money and you do me a favor, the prosecutor has to prove that you did me a favor *because* of the money.

So, corruption is definitely illegal in the United States, but it is also, at least in federal law, very hard to prove.

It may be that your organization wants to do more than evade prosecution and engage in activities that are *not necessarily criminal*. Perhaps it has higher ambitions.

Peach[1] set out three levels of responsibility:

Level one: **Basic**

- Pay taxes
- Observe the law
- Deal fairly

Level two: **Organizational**

- Minimize negative effects
- Act in the spirit of the law

Level three: **Societal**

- Responsibility for a healthy society
- Help remove or alleviate society's ills and problems

---

[1] Peach, L. 1987. "Corporate Responsibility." In *Effective Corporate Relations,* ed. Hart, N. Maidenhead: McGraw Hill.

We will be returning to this model, but consider it here in the context of corruption. You can, of course, simply decide to obey whatever laws are applicable in your jurisdiction. Perhaps, that is the only anti-corruption policy an organization needs. But, even at this minimal level, there is a need to engage in training to make sure that decision makers understand what the law actually requires.

Can a Business Succeed in Some Markets *Without* Corruption?

If a business decides to go further than simply obeying the letter of the law and maintain a rigorous policy against corruption, does that mean losing out on some contracts?

Of course, it might. But, this will not always be the case.

Henri Deterding, founder of Royal Dutch Petroleum and, later, Royal Dutch Shell, laid down the rule, "Never pay baksheesh. Never." But, Shell operates in markets all over the world, with widely different traditions, cultures, and laws. Is it even possible to win contracts without paying bribes in some of these countries?

Occasionally, it is not, and Shell is willing to walk away from such contracts. But, there is also a way of winning in markets such as this. There is a case to be made, even to the most corrupt official, that being tough on corruption is a good thing. Shell does not pay bribes, but it does not take them either. Shell's subcontractors win contracts on merit.

If you are a corrupt official in the Republic of Volta, oil matters. It is very much in your interest that the contract to construct the rigs and the pipeline is awarded to competent contractors. Because oil exports bring dollars into the country, even the most corrupt official who views the national treasury as his own personal source of income sees the value of bringing in dollars. Without them, he or she is restricted to stealing the local currency.

What if No One Really Suffers?

In the United Kingdom and other Commonwealth realms such as Canada, Australia, and New Zealand, the Queen (always acting on the *advice* of the relevant Prime Minister) can hand out honors. These can be rewards for all sorts of services to the community: political, charity, entertainment, or business. Almost all of them are meaningless and confer no actual power, but give the recipient the right to be known as John Smith OBE (Order of the British Empire) or Sir John Smith. Sometimes these awards are given to political donors. Why not? Politics is an important part of the community.

But, the one thing that is absolutely not supposed to happen is that there should be an explicit *quid pro quo.* No one is supposed to agree to give money to a political party *in exchange* for an honor.

That does not mean it has never happened. British Prime Minister David Lloyd George (1863–1945, PM 1916–22) was fairly open about this. There was an explicit price list.

It is certainly possible to argue that largely meaningless honors such as this are a great way of encouraging people to give time or money to worthy causes. In France and Italy, it is open, and widely accepted, that donations to political parties get you contracts from the government agency—whether it is central government or the city council. In America, party donors can be appointed to government positions such as ambassadorships. Joseph Kennedy, for example, was a major donor to the Democratic Party in the 1930s and was appointed to the prestigious role as ambassador to the United Kingdom. There are protections in the United States against abuse of this system. Ambassadors—and many other appointments—need to be approved by the Senate, so any wholly inappropriate nomination could be blocked.

But, let us imagine you are Prime Minister of a Commonwealth Realm. You have a reputation as a *pretty decent sort of guy.* You would never make an explicit agreement to give someone an honor in exchange for a donation to your party—let alone to you personally. But a somewhat shady businessman offers you a deal. He will make a very large donation to a charity that builds wells and provides goats to villages in developing countries, but only if you make an explicit promise to give him a knighthood.

In the wider scheme of things, a knighthood does not matter. He gets to call himself Sir Roger Businessman, not Mr. Roger Businessman. But, those wells and goats really do matter.

But, an explicit arrangement like this, that is corruption, isn't it? Do you accept the deal?

Drury, Krieckhaus, and Lusztig (2006)[2] define corruption "as the abuse of public office for private gain." Is that satisfactory? It follows Nye (1967):[3] "Corruption is behaviour which deviates from the formal duties of a public role because of private-regarding (personal, close family, private clique) pecuniary or status gains; or violates rules against the exercise of certain types of private-regarding influence."

These definitions put a stress on the *public* role or office. Is bribing the CEO of a business not corruption then?

In considering this, perhaps we need to consider recent (2019) discussions in the United States about wealthy individuals, including celebrities, pulling strings to get their children into top-rated universities. In the United States, some highly regarded universities, such as Harvard and Stanford, are private institutions. On the other hand, the University of California is a state institution. If it is corrupt for someone to bribe their way into the University of California at Berkeley, is it less so to use the same means to get into Harvard?

Ian Senior (2006)[4] offers a different definition: "Corruption occurs when a corruptor (1) covertly gives (2) a favour to a corruptee or to a nominee to influence (3) action(s) that (4) benefit the corruptor or a nominee, and for which the corruptee has (5) authority." He argues that

---

[2] http://sites.asiasociety.org/asia21summit/wp-content/uploads/2010/11/Corruption-Democracy-EconomicGrowth.pdf (accessed September 29, 2019).

[3] Nye, J.S. 1967. "Corruption and Political Development: A Cost–Benefit Analysis." *American Political Science Review* 66, no. 2, p. 417.

[4] https://iea.org.uk/wp-content/uploads/2016/07/upldbook324pdf.pdf (accessed September 29, 2019).

all five of the conditions must be met for something to be considered *corruption*.

An open arrangement, therefore, such as open donations to a political campaign, is not corruption, unless there is an explicit, and covert, promise.

The word *benefit* there would, because it is a necessary component of this definition of corruption, would exclude a promise made for a donation to charity, rather than to the official or a family member. Neither the official nor the official's family benefits from such a donation. (At least, typically. It could, possibly, involve a donation to a charity providing expensive medical treatment for a condition from which a member of the official's family happens to suffer.)

Senior classifies corruption as the *world's Big C*. The comparison with cancer is explicit and deliberate. Cancer corrupts the cells of a living body, causing them to grow uncontrollably and in a way that is harmful to the host organism.

In the eulogy for his father (Malcolm Langley, 1920–2017), this author said that corruption "corrodes cooperation and sows cynicism." By undermining the trust that makes cooperation possible, corruption undermines the very thing that makes us human. Without the ability to cooperate on complex problems, humans are just naked, and largely defenseless, apes.

If corruption is really that serious, then aren't arguments about its definition beside the point? If arrangements that are covert in the United States are conducted openly in the Republic of Volta, or some other fictional African country, are they surely just as damaging for being open?

Not quite.

Consider, for a moment, the role of corruption in the media. If a business bribes a journalist for favorable coverage of a product launch in the United States, then the arrangement would certainly be covert. That is not how journalism is supposed to work in the United States. Yet, this author has been offered—and has firmly declined—offers of favorable coverage in exchange for money in other countries. The journalists are often puzzled. How could I have expected to get coverage without paying? That is how these things are done.

There is a strong case for saying such arrangements are wrong and corrupt and should always be declined, wherever they happen to be. But, they are not the same. If an American journalist took such a payment, then the harms to others are explicit. Businesses that behaved honorably would be disadvantaged by comparison. Readers would be deceived.

But, in a context where such payments are expected, this is far from clear. No one objects to businesses receiving advertisements in exchange for payment, precisely because this is open and expected. If readers know that editorial coverage too is bought and sold, then they have not been deceived.

The loss is at a more subtle level.

Senior argues that one of the preconditions for endemic corruption is a lack of transparency. If corruptors corrupt the media, then they create an environment for more corruption.

Dilemmas

These dilemmas come from Hampden-Turner and Trompenaars (1993).[5]

Choose between the following statements:

1. A company's only goal is to make a profit
2. In addition to making a profit, seeking the well-being of various stakeholders:

% only profit: United States 40; Australia 35; Canada 34; United Kingdom 33; It 28; Sweden 27; the Netherlands 26; Belgium 25; Germany 24; France 16; Singapore 11; Japan 8.

You run a large department; a sub-ordinate with problems at home is frequently late. What right has he to expect your protection?

% saying "no right": United States 95; Germany 94; Sweden 91; United Kingdom 84; the Netherlands 82; Australia 82; Canada 81; Singapore 61; Belgium 57; Japan 56; Italy 47; France 43.

You are hiring. Should the new person principally be someone who fits in or who has the skills, knowledge, and record of success:

---

[5] Hampden-Turner, C., and Trompenaars, F. 1993. *The Seven Cultures of Capitalism: Value Systems for Creating Wealth in the United States, Japan, Germany, France, Britain, Sweden, and the Netherlands*. Doubleday Business.

% saying skills: United States 92; Aus 91; Can 91; NL 88; Ger 87; UK 71; Be 69; It 62; Fra 57; Swe 53; Jap 49; Sin 39.

If I apply for a job in a company:

(a) I will most certainly work there for the rest of my life
(b) I am almost sure the relationship will have a limited duration

Proportion saying limited duration:

- US 99%; Can, Aus 96%; UK 94%
- NL 89%; Ger 84%; Swe 81%
- Fra 79%; It 72%; Bel 71%
- Jap 41%
- Sin 32%

Pay particular attention to that last split. Unlike some of the others, there's a clear Anglosphere, Europe, Asia, split. This says something about the way people see a company as part of a community, rather like family. In western countries, there is a clear divide between professional and family lives.

Perhaps, the strong loyalty to a company in Asia makes corruption less likely. But perhaps, the separation lets people see a distinction between family duty and corporate duty.

In some countries, it is perfectly normal to take visiting business contacts—perhaps sales representatives from a supplier company—to meet to your family. Does that seem as though it is a good way of doing business?

Misangyi, Weaver, and Elms[6] argue that corruption is driven, in part, by the *institutional logic* of different organizations. They cite the argument in Soviet dominated economies prior to 1989 that those who fail to steal from their employers are stealing from their families. This notion seems

[6] Misangyi, V., Weaver, G., and Elms, H. 2008. "Ending Corruption: The Interplay Among Institutional Logics, Resources, and Institutional Entrepreneurs." *Academy of Management Review* 33, no. 3, pp. 750–770.

to be the opposite of the notion of long-term loyalty to an employer, which we see in Asian societies. Yet, it is possible that the Soviet societies were rather different. Government, both as an employer and as an arbiter of law, may have been seen as illegitimate. It was not democratically elected, may have been seen in occupied countries—perhaps including the non-Russian republics of the Soviet Union itself—as *foreign*. It is not hard to imagine Polish workers saying that of course they would steal from the Russian occupation forces, and they had stolen from the Germans during the Nazi occupation too. Legitimacy of government may be a key factor in fighting corruption. Misangyi et al. focused much of their research on reforms in Bosnia-Herzegovina, formerly part of the equally multinational state of Yugoslavia.

Misangyi et al. suggest that one way to combat corruption is to make the case that society as a whole is damaged by corruption. You would be better off living in a less corrupt society. This runs the risk—assuming you can persuade people of the merits of your case—of hitting what economists call the *tragedy of the commons*. You would certainly be better off if *everyone else* was less corrupt but not if you are the only person to give it up. Perhaps, it would be more effective to ensure that staff understand the role of the organization and their role in making the organization work. This type of *motivational framing* is also one of their recommendations.

Societies with a good record of combating corruption typically have low social and legal tolerance of corrupt behavior and robust structures for discovering and punishing it. Generally speaking, they are open societies with free media. So, which are the best countries at combating corruption?

Every year, Transparency International compiles a Corruption Perceptions Index, which is designed to measure the levels of corruption across markets around the world.

Typically, countries such as Denmark, New Zealand, Finland, and Singapore score very highly. North Korea, Yemen, Syria, South Sudan, and Somalia tend to appear toward the bottom.

The United States has recently fallen out of the top 20.

But, some of the results are not as predictable as you might imagine. Botswana and Bhutan score better than some European countries, including Poland, Spain, and Italy.

Corruption is an extremely serious problem. Senior concluded:

Using regression analysis and taking Transparency International's Corruption Perceptions Index 2004 as the dependent variable, the author tests fourteen independent variables for statistical significance as possible causes of corruption. Those that proved significant are: the prevalence of informal markets (more informal markets, more corruption); the respect for property rights (less respect, more corruption); the amount of regulation (more regulation, more corruption); press freedom (less freedom, more corruption); personal honesty (less honesty, more corruption); and religiosity (perhaps counter-intuitively, more church attendance being related to more corruption). A separate test showed a significant correlation between high corruption and low incomes per head.

These are correlations. But, which do you think are the *causal* factors? Does poverty cause corruption? Or, is it more the other way around? Lack of press freedom seems likely to be a key causal factor, and the growth of digital platforms and citizen journalism might be a critical weapon in combating it. Higher regulation is likely, again, to be a causal factor. There is no need to bribe an official to get your dog-walking license if dog-walking is not a licensed profession.

But, what could be the reason for religiosity correlating with corruption?

Practical Exercise

In groups, imagine you are advising the government of a country that is ranked toward the middle of Transparency International's Corruption Perceptions Index. The government thinks it will attract more inward investment if it can rise above neighboring countries on this index.

Consider some of the measures that a country might introduce to slowly rise up the index. Consider such things as law enforcement, education, training, and transparency.

Academic Exercise

Critically analyze the various definitions of corruption that have featured in this chapter and produce your own definition that synthesizes the best elements.

Resources

Transparency International's Corruption Perceptions Index:
https://transparency.org/cpi2019
https://transparency.org/cpi2012/in_detail

CHAPTER 4

History and Accountability

> **The Ship of Theseus**
>
> Theseus was an ancient Athenian hero and adventurer. So, let us imagine that Theseus returns from his journey, and the Athenians decide to preserve his ship as a memorial and as a tourist attraction.
>
> Preserving it is easier said than done. The wood begins to rot. So, slowly, parts of the hull are replaced. The prow, the stern, the masts, and the decking all follow.
>
> There comes a time when every single part of the ship has been replaced, at least once.
>
> So, is this the same ship?
>
> What if the rotten planks were kept in a junkyard, and then a means of restoring them was discovered? What if the ship was reassembled from its original parts?
>
> Is this the Ship of Theseus too? So, now there are two ships. Are they both the original?
>
> This is one of the oldest problems in philosophy. Plato wrote about the Ship of Theseus, and Heraclitus once observed that you cannot cross the same river twice. It is different water, you see? Erosion and accumulation mean the banks are not in precisely the same place either. Nor is the riverbed. So, is it the same river?

A great many businesses have been accused of all sorts of horrible crimes against humanity. There were businesses that collaborated with the Nazis, for example, and others that participated in the slave trade.

It is obviously necessary, when talking about such events, to be careful with the timeline. We must avoid judging people anachronistically. If someone were to tell you, for example, that Joseph Kennedy, patriarch of the American political dynasty, admired Hitler and expressed sympathy for his handling of Jewish people, you would be horrified. But, Kennedy said this in 1938, before Kristallnacht, or the Wannsee conference that planned the Holocaust. It was already obvious by 1938 that Hitler was deeply anti-Semitic—as was Kennedy—but when Kennedy made those statements, he was not, and could not possibly have been, talking about genocide.

In the same way, IBM supplied the Third Reich with a punch card system for use in the census. The same system was later used—together with information gathered from the census—to plan the Holocaust. But, it is as absurd to blame IBM for the Holocaust as it is to blame Kennedy.

Bayer, which was then part of I G Farben supplied the Zyklon B gas for the Nazi extermination camps. It also employed slave labor from the camps. Now, we are getting closer to a level of culpability.

Volkswagen was, effectively, formed by the Third Reich. Cars were very expensive in inter-war Germany, and the government wanted cheap cars to be made available to the people. *Volkswagen* literally means *peoples car.* So, there were certainly significant links between the company and the government of the Third Reich.

Did Volkswagen do something wrong here?

It was collaborating with the internationally recognized government of Germany. And, of all Nazi policies, the objective of cars that ordinary people could afford does not seem to be the most heinous.

In post-communist countries, especially those of the former Soviet Union and its satellites, many of the early politicians were former communists. Of course, most people holding professional jobs, and all people in senior government positions during the communist years, were communists. We were faced with the spectacle of people arguing about the morality of the precise date on which people left the Communist Party.

There are dozens, maybe hundreds, of American businesses that were trading in the antebellum years, when slavery was a major component of the economy in several states. There are banks and other financial institutions that insured slave owners against loss or damage to their *"property"* or even loaned money using slaves as collateral. In principle—and no doubt, on occasion, in practice—banks could seize the slaves and sell them to pay off the loan. Some of those banks are still trading, or, at least, successor companies to them are. Several have decided to apologize for their role in this business.

They were, of course, operating entirely within the law, as it was then written. Does that mean it was okay? There is a second sin of anachronism. The first is judging people in accordance with what we know now, but they did not know at the time. The second is much grayer. Is it okay to judge people by ethical standards that are accepted today, but that were regarded quite differently in the past?

In trying to avoid judging people anachronistically, we need to exercise caution. While we cannot blame IBM for things that we know now, but that no one knew in the 1930s, but slavery in the antebellum South was completely out in the open.

Nor was it something that was universally accepted, at least not by the 1860s. Centuries earlier, it had been. Literally no one in the Bible condemns slavery as immoral. Were they, therefore, all immoral people?

The majority of American states immediately prior to the Civil War did *not* allow slavery. Most European countries did not allow it. There had been campaigns for its abolition for 200 years.

It may be too much to condemn the disciples of Jesus for not being among the first people to attack slavery, but, by the 1860s, people who supported it were perfectly aware of the arguments. They knew that many people considered slavery wrong. Yet, they concluded that it was not.

In Biblical times, there was no debate about slavery. In the 1860s, there was, and Jefferson Davis and James Buchanan chose the wrong side.

The USS Minotaur

Captain Theseus of the USS Minotaur has been thinking a bit about the transporter. Every time he beams to a planet, it breaks him down to the molecular level and reconstructs him on the planet.

Is the new Captain Theseus on the planet the same one that was in the transporter room a few moments earlier? He feels the same. His memories are the same. And, that is how we define ourselves, isn't it? By our memories? But if all the atoms are different, is he really the same person?

Of course, every cell in his body has been replaced numerous times in the course of his life. Measured at the cellular level, he is not the *same* person as he was 20 years ago. But, for everything to change in a matter of seconds is disconcerting.

And, what if something went wrong? What if the transporter beam somehow split, with one-half bouncing back to its point of origin and the other continuing to its destination? He had heard of this happening once.[1] There would be two Captains Theseus. Which would be the *real* one? Or would they, somehow, both be real. What if his memories and thought processes could be broken down and downloaded onto a computer? Would the computer and any copies of the software also be the *real* Captain Theseus?

The abolition of slavery in the United States did not end racial disparity. There were *black codes* and segregation for another century. This was within living memory. Prominent African Americans of today had their lives directly marked by it. Barack Obama's parents would not have been allowed to be married or to cohabit in several states at the time of his birth. As a child, Condoleeza Rice moved with her family from Alabama to Colorado. The fact that young Condoleeza was an excellent student, plainly bound for higher education, was probably a factor, as the University of Alabama had only recently allowed any African American students at all.

We will discuss, in the next chapter, brands that have marked themselves out as virtuous and maybe won some brand loyalty by doing so. The Major League Baseball franchise, the Dodgers (now in LA, but formerly of Brooklyn) was the first to sign an African American player (Jackie Robinson, who had previously been playing in the *negro leagues*). But for every business that was ahead of the moral curve, there were others who were behind.

It is true that most businesses based in the Southern states could not be directly blamed for segregation. It was the law. They were not allowed

---

[1] Medlock, M.A. 1993. *Second Chances,* Season 6, Episode 24, *Star Trek: The Next Generation.*

to serve both black and white customers. While that does not mean that all business owners were desperate to integrate their businesses, it was the law precisely because *some* would have done so, if they had been allowed.

And what about voluntary organizations? The Democratic Party—the party of Jefferson Davis and James Buchanan—still exists. Has it done enough to be forgiven for slavery? What about the much more recent sin of segregation?

Let us consider, for a moment, the career of one of the elder statesmen of the party: 39th President, Jimmy Carter. Carter was born in 1924, and no one claims he is, or ever has been, a racist. No doubt, during his childhood, some office-holders of the Confederacy were still alive, but, when he came of age in 1945, the Civil War had been over for 80 years. There were still a few military veterans, from both sides, mostly teenaged conscripts, but anyone of any seniority was certainly dead.

But, segregation was still going strong. Carter probably did not like it, but many of his friends and supporters in Georgia certainly did. Indeed, in 2019, former Vice President Joe Biden remarked that when he had first joined the Senate (in the 1970s), it was still run by old segregationists.

Every plank of wood in the Democratic Party's Ship of Theseus has been replaced since slavery, but not since segregation. The same goes, of course, for businesses that operated in the Deep South.

There is an active debate in American politics as to whether African Americans deserve to be compensated for slavery, and perhaps also for segregation.

Certainly, there are governments—federal, state, and city—and businesses, and voluntary organizations that have a clear continuity of existence since the time of slavery. Every single person has been replaced, but the organizations still exist.

Should they be held liable? Liability does not disappear because the board of directors changes. The national debt does not get canceled when a new president is elected. Liability can certainly survive beyond the terms of office of those who incurred the debt.

Should the descendants of slaves be compensated? Should the still living victims of segregation be compensated? Should that include white business owners who lost money because they were forced to turn away black customers? Georgetown University is seeking to contact the descendants of slaves the university once owned and compensate them.

Just how long of a time has to pass before an organization that was involved in something that we now consider unethical can be forgiven?

And, should we, in any case, be judging people by what we *now* consider unethical, or should we be looking at the context of the time?

Obviously, businesses that did not know—and could not have known—that their products would be used in the Holocaust are innocent. But, how do we judge businesses that knew about segregation, something that was widely supported in some American states, while being regarded as totally immoral in others?

The Nazi Experiments Dilemma

Let us suppose that you are a medical researcher seeking to find the best way to resuscitate people suffering from hypothermia. Is it best to give people blankets and allow them to warm up naturally (passive warming)? Or, is it more effective to actively warm people by exposing them to a heat source such as a radiator or hot fluids? Experimentation is very difficult in this field. Each patient you encounter is unique. They have been exposed for different lengths of time. Their core body temperatures will be different.

Of course, it would be grossly unethical to expose people to hypothermia deliberately by, for example, putting large numbers of people into tanks of ice water to measure how long it would take them to die and to see which resuscitation techniques work best. Fortunately, you do not have to. The Nazis did it for you.

The hypothermia tests were among many despicable tortures administered at the Nazi death camps of Auschwitz, Dachau, Buchenwald, and Sachsenhausen. The data gathered in these experiments are unique. No one has conducted similar experiments before or since, and presumably never will again. There is simply no way to get this data without gross ethical breaches.

So, is it okay to *use* the data?

In 1988, Doctor Robert Pozos of the Hypothermia Laboratory at the University of Minnesota proposed to publish the data from these experiments, with his analysis and commentary, in the esteemed *New England Journal of Medicine*. The Journal's editor, Doctor Arnold Relman, flatly refused.

Of course, some of the Nazi experiments were utterly compromised scientifically, because they were premised on Nazi racial theory. They were all compromised ethically, because the subjects were not volunteers, and the methodology of the experiment was, at least, very dangerous and was sometimes literally designed to kill and measure how long it took people to die.

But, in the case of an experiment that is ethically compromised, but genuinely discovered something new, is it more ethical to ignore the data or to use it?

If the data are ignored, then we are sacrificing the one good thing that could possibly have come from the experiments, and future patients will die, even though we had access to knowledge that could have saved them.

If the data are used, then we have conceded that one good thing *did* come from the experiments. And, just maybe, someone will try something like this again in the future.

What is the right approach?

Here is another unethical experiment.

Let us suppose you are a doctor and you have a viable theory that might lead to the prevention of a highly contagious disease with a very high mortality rate. Millions are dying from it. So, you try your preventative treatment on a young boy. *Then, you deliberately expose him to the disease.*

That is pretty horrifying. But, it has happened. Fortunately, the boy was fine. Edward Jenner had demonstrated that exposure to cowpox immunized people to smallpox. The entire science of immunology was born. Jenner has been credited with saving more lives than anyone else in human history.[2]

If we examine this by utilitarian standards, then Jenner's experiment was clearly right. Hundreds of millions of people have benefited

---

[2] https://atlantichealthpartners.com/immunization-insights-1/2015/7/9/meet-the-man-credited-with-saving-more-lives-than-any-other (accessed September 11, 2019).

from vaccines, and not just the vaccine against smallpox, a disease that has been eliminated, but hundreds of other diseases too. The boy was unharmed, but the whole point of the experiment was that Jenner did not know the boy would be unharmed.

Kant's *categorical imperative,* which places Jenner's experiment in category of wrong things, may seem to be a better guide than utilitarianism on this occasion.

If we are boycotting Nazi experiments, should we boycott immunology too? Fortunately, the effectiveness of vaccines has been confirmed by many other experiments that have been validly and ethically conducted. But, it all started with Jenner.

American courts adopt a doctrine called "fruit of the poisoned tree." This means that if police conduct an illegal search, not only is the product of that search inadmissible as evidence, but any further evidence uncovered because of something gleaned from the illegal search is also inadmissible. The entire science of immunology is fruit of Edward Jenner's poisoned tree. The science is valid, but was kickstarted by an unethical experiment.

Practical Exercise

Debate the motion:

This House Believes the U.S. Federal Government Should Pay Reparations for Slavery.

Note, you can vary this by putting businesses, voluntary organizations, or the states in place of the federal government or by using segregation instead of slavery.

Consider the question of who pays—current taxpayers or shareholders, who were not involved, but also who receives the money. Has anyone now alive actually suffered from legal slavery?

Academic Exercise

Write an academic reflection on what you have learned preparing for and participating in the debate.

Use some of the formal academic reflection models such as those of Bereiter and Scardamalia (1993), Kolb (1984), or Chinn and Kramer (1995). (There are many more.)

For freshmen students, I specify using at least one of the reflection models. For more experienced students, I specify using at least two models and then reaching an integrated conclusion, which draws on the learning from both reflections.

CHAPTER 5

Corporate Social Responsibility

Corporate social responsibility (CSR) is a self-regulating business model that helps a company be socially accountable—to itself, its stakeholders, and the public.

—Investopedia

Corporate social responsibility (CSR) is how companies manage their business processes to produce an overall positive impact on society. It covers sustainability, social impact and ethics, and done correctly should be about core business—how companies make their money—not just add-on extras such as philanthropy.

—MallenBaker.net

When writing about Corporate Social Responsibility (CSR) many commentators use the phrase *enlightened self-interest.*

A business has owners, and, ultimately, the owners will decide how a business is run. They may be seeking to maximize profits. They may have a quite different objective, such as changing society. They may not see a conflict between the two.

There is no doubt that great many businesses have changed society, whether or not that was their objective. As Smith pointed out (see Chapter 1), the business owner is guided as though by *an invisible hand* to provide good customer service to maximize profits, but it can work the other way too.

Henry Ford set out to make money. He realized that manufacturing motor cars very cheaply and paying his workers well would lead to Ford workers becoming Ford customers. The spread of the motor car has had profound social impacts across the industrialized world.

A clear-thinking business owner realizes that there are many reasons to take account of the views of other stakeholders in the business. Yes, of course, you listen to customers. But, well-motivated staff and low staff turnover can improve business performance. Loyal investors make it easier for the business to borrow money. Supportive neighbors and communities can buoy a company through difficult times and support the relationship with politicians and regulators, who are often the main driver of profitability.

Unweaving the Rainbow

Starbucks founder Howard Schultz has been outspoken in supporting gay partner benefits for Starbucks staff. (Confusingly, Starbucks calls its staff "partners"). While there's now widespread support for gay marriage in the United States, this has not always been so.

In the 1990s, Congress overwhelmingly passed the Defense of Marriage Act that defined marriage as the union of one man and one woman. Even liberal states such as Washington and California (twice) voted in popular initiatives against recognizing gay marriage. But Starbucks continued to offer benefits, such as health coverage and pensions, to the partners of its gay staff. Why?

No doubt Schultz felt passionately about the issue. But if his customers were strongly against the idea, why did he stick to it?

Of course, Starbucks customers may not have been against the idea. Everyone can vote in a popular initiative, but not everyone is a customer of Starbucks. Its locations are mostly urban. Its customers are likely to be younger than the average of the United States, and, given its reputation as a place to hang out, perhaps more likely to be single. These factors all correlate with a more liberal customer base than for a rural chain themed around Country Music.

But Disney has been offering gay partner benefits since before Starbucks was even founded. It began before Congress even discovered a

---

"need" to pass the Defense of Marriage Act. Some religious organizations even backed campaigns to get people to boycott Disney. The company's customer base is mostly families with young children, a group in which gay people are unlikely to be overrepresented.

So why did Disney do it?

Are there any stakeholders likely to care more about staff benefits than customers do? How well represented are gay people likely to be among the singers, actors, and dancers that Disney needs to recruit?

But, of course, businesses can affect society in negative ways too. An obvious example is pollution. Pollution can be regulated in all sorts of different ways, a few of which create incentives to avoid it.

Of course, businesses can be sued for pollution that they cause. But, this is not always effective for many reasons. For example, sometimes, the damage from pollution is caused to unowned property, such as the high seas. As no one owns the ocean, no one has standing to sue, but that does not mean there has been no damage.

Sometimes, people are unaware of the damage. People may fall ill only some time after long exposure to a pollutant. They may not be aware of the connection, or they may suspect a connection that they cannot prove.

Sometimes, the damage is spread out over many people and may be trivial to each of them. This is known as salami-slicing or perhaps the *Gus Gorman* approach, after the character in Superman III who becomes rich by stealing one cent from every bank account in America.

Sometimes businesses are able to pressure politicians into giving them permission to pollute or immunity from lawsuits.

Broadly speaking, CSR can be seen as encompassing a range of key areas:

- Protecting the environment or animal welfare
- Preventing discrimination and harassment
- *Fair trade* or ensuring good labor practices in the supply chain
- Promoting integrity
- Philanthropic elements or charity

Priorities on these issues vary between individuals, from country to country and over time. Generally speaking, people are more focused on jobs and labor issues when the economy is doing poorly and on environmental issues when the economy is doing well. In western countries, people are more concerned about the environment than in developing countries, where the focus is often on ensuring that products are safe and reliable.

Case Study – Primark

(Data from: BusinessCaseStudies.co.uk)

The value clothing retailer, Primark, was founded in Ireland, and, by 2012, it had 238 branches across Europe (including United Kingdom and Ireland). Primark is not a manufacturer: its products are largely sourced from Asia. sourcing includes countries such as Turkey, India, Bangladesh, and China. The brand promotes its responsibility agenda to keep internal and external stakeholders engaged.

Primark supports HERProject (Health Enables Returns) that works with Primark and its suppliers, including in Bangladesh.

In Bangladesh, 50 percent of the manufacturing workforce is female—often with little education. There are low levels of literacy. As a result, knowledge of health, nutrition, and hygiene is low.

HERProject

Because of poor hygiene, infections are widespread and childbirth is especially hazardous. This, of course, has been the case for most women throughout most of history, but is much less the case today in countries with education and clean water supplies.

HERProject sees education as the key to combatting this. Ten percent of female employees were selected as "peer group educators", trained to teach others.

Umme Habiba (garment worker):

'The trainers told me that many diseases come from the unpurified water that I was taking from the tap. This water can be the cause of sickness, cholera and diarrhea. At first myfamily said to me, how do you know this stuff? You work in a garments factory! I told them it's what I have learnt from the HERproject. When I began to give them advice they started to get interested in the project. Everyone I have told now boils their water and they don't suffer like before.'

Return on Investment

Obviously, people will see this as a worthwhile ethical policy. It is also good business practice. Factories with Primark investments in HER-Project report:

- improvements in productivity
- a more stable workforce
- lower absenteeism
- decreased labor turnover
- improved quality and a reduction in housekeeping costs

One factory MD in Bangladesh could put figures on this:

- Absenteeism was down 55 percent in the first six months of HERProject's work
- Turnover of female workers fell from 50 to 12 percent

Mrs. Kaniz Fatema (factory manager):

"HERproject has made a real difference in my factory. The workers have increased their productivity as they are now looking after themselves better. I have become a lot closer to my female workers. I have also told other factory managers about the success of the project at our factory. The male workers are now asking when we will start a similar project for them."

Rana Plaza

In April 2013, the Rana Plaza building in Savar, Bangladesh, collapsed. Workers were making clothes for western retailers, including Primark.

- 1,129 killed, 2,515 injured
- Deadliest garment factory collapse in history
- Deadliest accidental structural failure in modern times
- Within days, there were protests outside Primark's Oxford Street store

Response

Primark paid over 14 million U.S. dollars to the victims of the collapse. The fund was administered by the International Labour Organization (ILO).

Primark was an early funder, and its support was used to pressurize other retailers that had been using the Rana Plaza factory as a supplier.

As the Primark case study suggests, even businesses that invest in trying to clean up their supply chain can encounter problems and come in for criticism. Indeed, it may be that the more loudly a business proclaims its ethical strategy, the more it will encounter a backlash if something does go wrong. In this case, it concerned the health and safety of workers in the supply chain, but it could as easily have concerned the environment, animal welfare, or any one of a number of issues.

What if Whole Foods turned out to have been using factory farms to supply its animal-based products? This would be an existential challenge for the brand. People may not expect high animal welfare standards from McDonald's—although the company does claim to monitor such things—but they do have high expectations of Whole Foods, and the issues matter to Whole Foods customers. Ultimately, customers of McDonald's may value its work with Ronald McDonald House, but it is not the reason they choose the brand. Whole Foods customers, by contrast, probably value the business's ethical stand very highly. It could well be a brand-switching issue for many of them.

So, how should a business construct its CSR policy?

It is time to revisit Peach:

Peach[1] set out three levels of responsibility:

Level one: Basic

- Pay taxes
- Observe the law
- Deal fairly

Level two: Organizational

- Minimize negative effects
- Act in the spirit of the law

Level three: Societal

- Responsibility for a healthy society
- Help remove or alleviate society's ills and problems

---

[1] Peach, L. 1987. "Corporate Responsibility." In *Effective Corporate Relations,* ed. Hart, N. Maidenhead: McGraw Hill.

This choice is a strategy. Not all businesses will go beyond the minimum, and those that do would not be marking themselves out if everyone did.

Consider, for a moment, the situation of a business that is using its stance on, say, animal welfare to mark itself out. Customers, employees, and other stakeholders may be proud to be associated with the company because of this stance. But, what if the standard that this company upholds then becomes law? Suddenly, all the business's competitors will be upholding the same standard. Of course, for a time, there is an opportunity to proclaim that you are pleased that everyone else is coming into line. You can proclaim yourself as a trendsetter. But, down the line, this selling point, which has persuaded people to choose you, loses its potency. Either you need to find a new selling point or you need to raise the bar again and commit yourself to still higher standards than those you have hitherto observed and by which all your competitors are now bound.

So, how does a business decide what to prioritize in its CSR strategy? Let us say that you have decided you want to go further than the legal minimum and have a clear statement of your values. What are the values? Often, this is influenced by the vision of the founder—Howard Schultz at Starbucks, say—but maybe the business is seeking a new statement, years after the founding.

This author wrote a CSR statement for real estate firm, Knight Frank (now known as Newmark Knight Frank in the United States). What was the key point?

For a firm advising clients on real estate, integrity of advice, fair dealing, and professional standards were at the heart of the statement. The author had previously worked at Shell, where environmental issues were necessarily predominant.

For some businesses, the core business is inherently linked to a key social concern: for example, energy companies and the environment. While all businesses have an environmental footprint, and contribute in some way to pollution, for many, there is no impact beyond the very general focus on energy conservation or recycling. There is nothing a real estate firm needs to do on this issue over and above what would be expected of any business. (We are speaking here of real estate agency, of course. A construction company certainly makes key environmental decisions in its design and materials choices.)

So, energy companies will highlight the environment in particular. Fashion companies will focus on sourcing decisions and how they impact both the environment and working conditions in supplier companies. Some—those dealing in leather, fur, and other animal products, perhaps even including silk—will probably want to address animal welfare concerns.

Certainly, businesses can choose causes that are only very loosely related to their core business. In the United States, there is a long tradition of corporate philanthropy, from the Rockefellers and Carnegies to Bill Gates and Mark Zuckerberg. Businesses can acquire a *halo* effect by associating themselves with any type of good cause.

Which cause would you choose for some of the following brands?
KPMG
T-Mobile
Manchester United
Toyota
Madonna
Costco
Tommy Hilfiger
Jet Blue
Visit Mauritius
Siemens
Johnson and Johnson
Nestle
Harvard
Google
Chick-Fil-A
Apple

This is where we revisit the ideas of Immanuel Kant, mentioned in Chapter 1. Kant[2] saw ethical behavior as a categorical imperative. Life, according to Kant, is a constant struggle between duty and pleasure.

---

[2] Kant, I. 1785. *Groundwork of the Metaphysic of Morals*. Riga: Johann Friedrich Hartknoch.

Potentially, a business will face the same struggle: between, for example, keeping costs low and keeping environmental or animal welfare standards high. Different businesses will choose different strategies, because customers and other stakeholders have different priorities. It is important to Wal-Mart to deliver low costs, because Wal-Mart customers value low prices. Whole Foods customers, by contrast, value organic production methods, animal welfare, and protection of the environment. Nobody goes to Whole Foods to save money, and the store has been nicknamed *Whole Paycheck.*

CSR practitioners use the language of *duty* and *rights* to promote strong CSR practices, but a for-profit business will always want to see a business case. Will customers, or other stakeholders, actively choose a business because of CSR? Can we win new customers, or enhance customer loyalty? Enlightened self-interest is still self-interest.

The board of directors will not want you to present them with Kant's conflict. Do not ask them to choose between profits and principles. Present a plan that shows the business can earn profits by implementing its principles.

Increasingly, businesses are at least nodding in the direction of *triple bottom line* accounting: reporting on a business's impact on *profit, people, and planet.* Shell published an externally audited report on the triple bottom line for the first time in the late 1990s, and this is now expected of businesses quoted on the London Stock Exchange and other international securities markets.

Where, then, does this leave Friedman's position described in Chapter 1 that managers owe responsibility to the owners of the business? He did not set out competing responsibilities to staff, the environment, or other groups.

R. Edward Freeman, considered the father of stakeholder theory, defined a stakeholder as "any group or individual who can affect or is affected by the achievement of the organization's objectives."[3]

Freeman's theory is expressly normative. He, and perhaps especially his followers, are presenting an argument about how a business should

---

[3] Freeman, R.E. 1984. *Strategic Management: A Stakeholder Approach.* New York: HarperCollins.

be run. The word *stakeholder* is not an accident. It is designed to echo the word *stockholder* and suggest that other groups should have similar rights with regard to running the business. It is about achieving a more *equitable* division of the rewards and power.

But, is there necessarily a conflict between the interests of the different groups? A corporation is a mechanism through which these diverse groups of people can cooperate. In a voluntary exchange, the business must pay all of the people who cooperate enough to secure their contribution.

There is nothing to prevent cooperatives of workers owning the business and paying interest to the suppliers of capital. Would that give the workers a more *equitable* share of the rewards? Friedman talks only of *owners* being in control, not investors. If workers are the owners then they set the objectives for the corporation.

It would not necessarily give them a greater share of the reward. The interest payments to those who loaned the capital would have to be made every month, whereas shareholders only draw when the business is trading profitably. It would be the workers, as owners, who would bear the risk in a downturn. Even if the workers earned as much overall—and they might not—it would be unevenly distributed over time, and they might not be able to withstand the cuts to their pay in difficult trading conditions.

Advocates for workers' cooperatives assume that workers prefer such an arrangement and would be more motivated. If that were so, then other things being equal, such cooperatives would attract the best staff, and this would be a competitive advantage. Cooperatives would grow in strength and investor-owned corporations would decline. So, we must assume either workers do not have such a preference—or at least not strongly so—or that other things are not equal.

Perhaps, cooperatives, with their democratic structures, are slow to make decisions. If so, this should be soluble. Workers, like investors, could elect boards and empower them to act decisively.

Perhaps then, most workers have no strong preference for employee-owned corporations, and any preference they do have for democratic governance is outweighed by a preference for the stability of wages over variable shareholder dividends.

If there is no reason to suppose that the division of rewards between workers and investors would be any different—let alone more *equitable*—is the difference between Friedman and Freeman more apparent than real?

Perhaps not. The amount that an investor-owned company pays to its employees—and, indeed, the amount an employee-owned company pays its investors—is set in contract. There are other stakeholders that do not have a contractual role.

Disney needs to provide the type of employment benefits that its employees demand to deliver for customers, and thus for stockholders, but not everyone affected by the decisions of the corporation can opt out.

Local communities, the flora and fauna of the local environment are not parties to any contract with the business and cannot withdraw from the contract if their needs are not being met. As we will see in Chapter 7, some people, let alone plants and animals, do not even know that they are affected by the decisions a corporation makes.

Corporations do not need the cooperation of people who are not contractually involved in the business (as customers, workers, or investors, for example) and may be inadvertently or unknowingly affected by, say, pollution.

But, such engagement can create exactly the ethical halo effect that some businesses set out to create. Loyalty from local communities can be an asset in times of crisis or political pressure. If a business is seen to be an ethical business, it may well have stronger loyalty from the stakeholders whose cooperation it does need. Loyal customers, investors, and staff are a clear competitive advantage in the marketplace.

So, businesses do not necessarily have to choose between generating returns for shareholders and engaging with other stakeholders. It is not a fixed pie to be divided between the different groups. An ethical, engaged, business might well be more successful and deliver more rewards to all its stakeholders.

The next chapters, covering discrimination and harassment (Chapter 6), animal welfare and the environment (Chapter 7), compliance and the culture of ethics (Chapter 8), and public safety (Chapter 9), draw out in much more detail the ethical issues involved in engaging these various stakeholders.

Practical Exercise

Giving endangered species a sporting chance

In 2017, Good, Burnham, and MacDonald[4] published research on the mascots of sports teams. Clubs with mammalian mascots playing in the 10 richest sports leagues in the world were the subject of the research. Of the mascots, 30 percent were endangered and 33 percent were critically endangered.

How much could these sports teams do to raise money or raise the profile of their endangered mascots? Think not only of how merchandizing can be used in fundraising, but how those high-profile sports stars can become public advocates, especially with the team's fanatically loyal followers?

Select a team and draw up a plan for actions it could take to help the endangered species.

Academic Exercise

Write an essay exploring the title: The environment is the most important element of CSR: we only have one planet.

Look at arguments that tend to support the proposition and arguments that tend to refute it. Reach a reasoned conclusion.

Resources

Freeman on Stakeholders: https://youtu.be/bIRUaLcvPe8

---

[4] Good, C.D., Burnham, D., and Macdonald, D.W. July, 2017. "A Cultural Conscience for Conservation." *Animals* 52, pp. 1–50.

CHAPTER 6

Harassment, Discrimination, and Inclusion

In preparing for a crisis, most organizations want to prepare for Scenario 1. Chemical companies want to prepare for a spill, a fire, a leak, or an explosion. Oil companies want to prepare for a tanker sinking or a rig leaking. Few people want to look past the obvious.

This is bad crisis preparation, of course. It is easy thing for which to prepare. If you are a chemical engineer, you are likely to know far more about chemistry than even the most aggressive journalist interviewing you. But, in omitting other crises, organizations are also committing an ethical failure. They are failing to comprehend their roles as, for example, employers.

In 2013, this author began campaigning to get clients to prepare for ethical crises that occur outside the core business and, in particular, for allegations of sexual harassment.

By 2017, it was clear that sexual harassment was going to be a very public issue for a number of employers. It was getting worldwide publicity in high-profile industries such as the media and entertainment sectors. It was slightly less obvious in sectors such as banking and the law, but many organizations—commercial, governmental, charitable—were beginning to realize that women are now more willing to speak out on these issues, and that is now a key risk factor as well as a critical ethical factor.

Being earlier than some to address this issue, this author has developed some teaching and training resources to confront it.

Everyone Knows He Is a Jerk[1]

The only woman in the executive leadership team arrives a little late for the meeting. All the chairs are occupied, so the CEO suggests that she sit on his lap. Ha Ha. Just one of the lads having a laugh.

He follows this by commenting that her dress looks good on her, but would look better on his floor. More laughter.

Later, she has a discussion with the COO, who tells her "everyone knows he's a jerk." The implication is that she should just live with it.

So, she approaches the board. After an emergency meeting, both the CEO and the COO get fired.

Is this the right reaction, or is this overkill?

Why was the COO fired? Did he do anything wrong?

In most common law jurisdictions, such as the United States, acknowledging that *everyone knows* about the problem immediately increases the organization's liability. Does this not seem fair? Organizations can certainly be liable for problems they did not know about; otherwise, there would be an incentive to avoid knowing. They are supposed to know. Sometimes, they are liable for things that they could not, even in theory, have known about, because someone has to bear that risk and the law says they do. But, it seems proper that their liability is greater if they knew.

When holding discussions in this scenario with students, there are two reactions that are predictable.

Someone (probably a woman) will say: "It depends what she was wearing."

Someone else (also, probably a woman): "No it doesn't. A woman has a right to wear anything she likes."

Who is right?

In a professional context, can a person (male or female) really wear anything? Or, are some modes of attire inappropriate?

If the woman in this scenario *was* dressed inappropriately (something on which we are given no information), did the CEO handle that

---

[1] Adapted from a scenario described in the *Wall Street Journal*.

in the most sensitive way? In those circumstances, what *should* he have done?

Perhaps, the better way of putting it is not that a woman can wear anything she likes, but that an employee should be treated decently whatever she or he is wearing. This focuses on the employer's duty to behave decently, not on the employee's right to wear any sort of clothing.

Once the board has begun the search for a new CEO and COO, what should it do next?

Should the board decide, as policy, that at least one of these positions should be held by a woman?

Should it organize an inquiry as to how this situation arose? If so, who should head it? Is the head of HR potentially compromised? Is the chief legal counsel? After all, *everyone* knew.

Perhaps, an outside lawyer or judge should be hired to run the inquiry.

Would it make sense to seek a woman for *that* role?

Typically, that question gets several responses:

Yes, definitely hire a woman.

No, someone qualified for the job. (But there are thousands of people qualified for this task, and a lot of them are women. It should not be hard to find someone who is both fully qualified and also female.)

No, a woman would be biased and just believe all the women.

Yes, the last one is a real response. On one occasion, it was raised by a West African student, so the follow-up question was obvious. What if he were the only black person in the senior leadership team and the CEO had made a racist joke instead? Would it be a good idea to find a black lawyer or a white lawyer to lead the investigation? He felt a black lawyer would be best. So what is the difference? Maybe, he conceded, a woman would be a good idea after all.

Overt harassment is only one issue that an organization can face. Does it have appropriate policies on hiring and recruitment? Is the culture appropriate to ensure fairness between races, sexes, and other protected categories in your jurisdiction?

You should note that if you operate in multiple jurisdictions, the law will differ from one to another, both about which categories are protected and how you are supposed to achieve fairness.

In most of the United Kingdom, religion is not a protected category unless it is a cover for racial discrimination, but in Northern Ireland, it is, partly because of a history of religious conflict and discrimination. Different jurisdictions have different histories, and the law reflects this.

In India, you need to be concerned about the traditional castes of South Asia.

In some jurisdictions, it is compulsory to have quotas for men and women, or for disabled people, or for races or castes. In others, quotas are illegal. A multinational organization will, therefore, be required to have different policies in different jurisdictions.

What if you think that your recruitment policies are race-blind and sex-blind, but that it so happens that all the best candidates are almost always white men?

If the law does not require, or even allow, quotas, does that mean you have done everything that you can and should do?

Quite possibly not. Just because you think your policies are non-discriminatory, it does not mean that they are.

An employer is looking to answer three questions about a candidate.

Can she do the job?
Will she do the job?
Will she fit in?

Even if you are skilled at assessing the first two, it may be that the third is where subconscious bias will slip in. If all of the people you currently have are white men, then it is easy to see white men fitting in. A tendency that may have begun innocently or by accident becomes self-reinforcing.

The traditional tool for assessing whether someone will fit in is the job interview. There is a lot of evidence that employers make up their minds about candidates within the first few seconds. The way you dress, your body language, smile, eye contact, and handshake are all key. By the time you sit down, the interview is over.

Employers do not know they do this. They will refer to things the candidate says during the interview when justifying their decision, but in practice, the decisions are made almost immediately. Multiple studies have shown that first impressions rarely change. One study[2] suggested that *naïve observers* could correctly predict the result of a job interview by experienced interviewers after viewing a video of the first 20 seconds of the interaction.

That is why, some governments monitor for apparent imbalances in the workforce, even where quotas are neither required nor legal. You may not be required to ensure that at least a quarter of your workforce is female, but if you fall short of this, you might be asked to explain why this is so.

And, shouldn't you, ethically, be asking this of yourself anyway? Maybe that final question is the problem. Perhaps, you should not be seeking someone who will *fit in*. In the preceding discussion (Everyone knows he's a jerk), the board would be expressly seeking someone to challenge the existing culture because the existing culture had just let the organization down. In terms of hiring the external consultant to review the culture, the *last thing* you want is someone who will *fit in*. Arguably, you should not want that in your new CEO and COO either.

What if you think your processes might well have structured, but unconscious, biases? How can you address these? Is it ethical, or lawful, to set a quota? If that is not allowed or does not seem like the right solution, there are other options.

You could incorporate some form of *objective assessment*. These are tests of skills and abilities or that classify people's personality types. You should be able to show a clear correlation between ability to do well on the tests and ability to do well in the job. Companies that sell these assessment techniques can provide that sort of evidence.

Other strategies include targeted recruitment or targeted hiring. Note here, the difference between recruitment and hiring and explore where the issue is in your organization.

---

[2] Prickett, T., N. Gada-Jain, F. Bernieari. May, 2000. "The Importance of First Impressions in a Job Interview." Presented at the Annual Meeting of the Midwestern Psychological Association, Chicago, IL.

Affirmative action *hiring* is setting out to hire people from underrepresented groups. Affirmative action *recruitment* is simply about encouraging people from those groups to apply for the jobs in the first place.

Affirmative action hiring will be impossible if people in the underrepresented groups do not apply for the jobs in the first place. But perhaps, you (legally) cannot or (ethically) will not engage in affirmative action hiring, but still want to expand your recruitment pool.

In the past, this meant buying ads in particular publications or channels. Now, advertising platforms such as Google and Facebook can help you engage in micro-targeting.

Is Affirmative Action **Hiring** Ethical?

Let us, for the moment, put aside the legal question. Let us assume you are operating in a jurisdiction where it is permitted, but not compulsory, so you are free to decide whether or not you want to engage in this hiring strategy.

Perhaps, the first thing to ask yourself is whether or not your organization is suffering any disadvantage by not hiring from the underrepresented group. If women or ethnic minorities are not applying for jobs at your organization, perhaps you are inadvertently giving a message that they are not welcome. If they feel unwelcome as employees, perhaps they feel unwelcome as customers too. You might be missing out on hiring some great candidates and also missing out on expanding your market.

If you can identify a problem that arises from lack of diversity and inclusion in your leadership team, then affirmative action can be a simple way of addressing it.

> **"They never run our press releases"**
>
> A few years ago, a friend of this author applied for a job at board level with a major automotive firm. She was to be the head of communications. She presented convincing data suggesting that most of the growth in new car sales over the coming decades would be to women. She wanted to get the company in women's magazines.
>
> The company was skeptical. "They never run our press releases," they responded. Of course not, she told them. Your press releases are

all about brake horsepower, torque, and performance. That is not how women choose cars.

The company, of course, was led by engineers, most of whom were men. They did not realize that men and women tend to approach decisions about cars differently.

Of course, these differences, real as they (apparently) are, are not absolute. They are akin to saying that men are taller than women. The average man is taller than the average woman, and the male bell curve for height is to the right of the female bell curve for height. And, this is where it can be easy to miss the distinction.

The women that the company did have in its senior leadership were mostly engineers with a strong interest in the automotive industry. They might well be interested in engine size and power—probably more than most men are—but it does not mean they are typical of women as a whole.

Such factors as style and safety are important to a lot of customers, including some men and most women, but not to the people in the senior leadership of the company. Or, at least, they did not see them as selling points. They recognized the value of safety, but did not believe customers chose models on that basis. We have all seen ads giving the time in which a car can go from 0 to 60 mph. How often do you see automakers boasting about how quickly a car can go from 60 to 0?

After being hired, our hero began to review all of the communication channels of the company. It turns out that some of the car showrooms were not well equipped. Buying a new car is a long and complex process. You may want to review several models and consider financing options. There may be a lot of paperwork to complete. There are important practical and comfort issues to consider.

For example, there was nowhere to change a baby and no play area for small children.

The sales team tended to make cold and unemotional presentations that focused on performance not functionality. They would offer coffee and tea in styrofoam cups. Some people—especially women—think that comes off as cheap. If you are spending tens of thousands of dollars, then the company can afford to offer you a china cup.

> Given both the length of time customers spend at the dealership, and the amount of money they are spending, little things can make a big difference, but the company had not even thought about them.
>
> So, here was a major company with a particular culture. Its leadership was made up of people who were enthusiastic for the product and its technical capabilities, without realizing that many customers see the product in a much more functional way. It is useful, rather than fun. Comfort, safety, and style may be more important than performance.
>
> Of course, this may have had more to do with culture than gender.
>
> If the company had set out to recruit more women, it might have ended up recruiting women who saw the product in same way the existing team did. People who would *fit in*. The leadership team might have looked different, but been culturally the same.
>
> So, challenging your recruitment and hiring demographics *may* be the disruption in thinking that you need, but it may not.

So, in setting diversity, discrimination, and harassment policies, an organization has a number of different tasks.

The first, per Peach (as discussed in other chapters), is to obey the law. This will vary between different jurisdictions.

Then comes the big question. *Why* are you concerned about diversity?

What value would it bring to your organization to have a more diverse workforce or a more diverse senior leadership team?

Your organization, undoubtedly, depends on a great many people, and not just its staff. It needs to attract customers. It needs to build support with investors. It may engage in outreach to neighbors and local communities. It may depend on political or regulatory decisions. Will it be able to handle those tasks more effectively if has a more diverse leadership?

This will vary from one organization to another. It will depend where you operate and what your core business is.

An obvious example in the United States is that an organization seeking a mass market needs to take account of the fact that a significant minority in the country is most comfortable speaking Spanish rather than English. Spanish speakers comprise a big slice of the consumer market in many states, including California, Texas, Florida, and New York—the four largest states by population.

But, not all organizations are in a mass market. Perhaps such niche organizations do not want to disrupt their core culture in the way that the automotive manufacturer discussed earlier did.

The Niche Player

Let us imagine that your business operates in a niche market. The team is about 20 people and never seems to expand or contract much. The CEO makes all the final hiring decisions and likes to hire people with whom he feels comfortable. Let us say the business gives investment advice to wealthy private clients.

The CEO went to a private high school and an elite university. A great many of the people he ends up hiring are quite a lot like him. They are clever, well educated, persuasive, and self-assured. They are mostly white and male.

He wants to hire women, of course. He interviews quite a few. He has hired some on occasion. But, it never seems to work out, and the people who stay long term are white men, usually from fairly elite social backgrounds and with an elite education.

But, the thing is, the clients seem to like this. Not all potential clients, of course, but enough. Things go up and down, but there is generally no shortage of work. These clever, self-assured people appeal to a certain sort of client, and those clients have plenty of business.

Should the business try to diversify in order to appeal to other clients? Or, will that put off some of the existing client base?

Would your answer be different if the company were one about the same size producing rap music and all the executives were black men instead of white men?

And, is there an *ethical* requirement on a medium-sized business, such as one of these to diversify?

What if we are talking about a huge, global business employing over 100,000 people? Is there an ethical case for that business to diversify?

And, if you are a white man looking to start a new business with a partner, should you seek a black woman, for balance?

How big does an organization have to be before its demographics become an ethical issue? Or, a practical one?

We considered, in Chapter 5, how issues relating to the LGBTQ community are relevant to a corporate social responsibility (CSR) campaign. Discrimination and harassment policies need to cover these issues too. Just as in other areas, the key difference is that discrimination and harassment are sometimes legal issues. Organizations can be accountable in civil, criminal, and administrative law for decisions that they make, and transnational companies will need to allow for different legal requirements in different markets. Over and above obeying the law, your organization may wish to position itself as taking a positive and progressive stance on issues in order to earn support and loyalty in your various stakeholder groups.

He said-she said

You are a divisional director in a large company. One afternoon, you receive two e-mails, one from a manager who reports to you and one from a member of his team.

The manager's e-mail contains an annual appraisal on the team member. It is unfavorable and describes her as not working well with others and difficult to manage.

The subordinate's e-mail is a disciplinary complaint against the manager. According to the complaint, the manager sexually propositioned his subordinate and said that he would give her a favorable appraisal and recommend her for a bonus if she complied, which she declined to do.

You speak to the manager, who denies her allegation and says that she had threatened to make a complaint against him if he did not promise a favorable appraisal. You ask why he did not log this on the appraisal. He replies that he probably should have, but did not believe she would go through with the threat.

Both are fairly new to your organization, and neither of them has a prior appraisal on record.

What actions would you take to investigate this matter?

What standard of evidence would you require?

In most European Union countries, any employee disciplinary matter needs to be investigated using criminal standards of proof: you would need evidence *beyond reasonable doubt* before you could discipline *either* party. In the United States, most states operate *at will* employment. You can sack either or both of the employees in just the same way you could sever a contract with a supplier: you would give the appropriate notice, but you are not required to provide a reason. (Any more than an employee is required to give a reason for quitting.) That said, dismissing someone on grounds of sex is illegal, and this could be problem in this instance.

What standard of proof do you think is reasonable before dismissing someone?

- "Beyond reasonable doubt" (used for criminal trials in common law jurisdictions)?
- "Preponderance of evidence" (used in most civil trials in common law jurisdictions)?
- "Clear and convincing evidence" (used in some civil trials and administrative court trials in the United States)?

Preponderance of evidence simply means more likely than not—a 51 percent chance. *Beyond reasonable doubt* is less clearly defined, but is sometimes related to the *Blackstone ratio* set out by English judge William Blackstone (1723–1780): **"It is better that ten guilty persons escape, than that one innocent suffer."**[3] That suggests at least 91 percent certainty.

Clear and convincing evidence is between the two. For example, in paternity cases, it is necessary to show that a given man is the father of child to a much higher standard than *preponderance of evidence*. It needs to be highly and substantially more probable than not.

In the case of Judge Brett Kavanaugh, he was not facing a criminal trial for attempted rape (where the standard would have been *beyond reasonable doubt*). He was not even facing employee disciplinary action—for example, being sacked as a judge. He was being considered for promotion from a district court to the United States Supreme Court.

---

[3] Blackstone, Sir William. 1765. *Commentaries on the Laws of England.* Oxford: Clarendon Press. Book IV, Chapter 27.

What standard of proof should the Senate have used when deciding whether or not to ratify his nomination by the President? The same as at any other job interview?

No CEO has ever said, "It is better that we hire ten rapists than that we refuse to hire one non-rapist". But criminal trial or not, the allegations against Kavanaugh were criminal and very public. His reputation would have been grievously damaged if he had been denied a promotion based on unproven criminal allegations.

Practical Exercise

Debate the motion:

This house believes that there should be affirmative action in university admissions.

Or, alternatively:

This house believes there should be a quota of at least 25 percent women on the boards of all public companies.

Academic Exercise

In groups, conduct a content analysis on Harvey Weinstein. Compare media reports about Weinstein in 2016 and in 2018.

You should tabulate the messages that the media included about Weinstein in each year and quantify how often each of these messages recurred.

Each member of the group should select a different news source. Consider entertainment, business and general media.

CHAPTER 7

Animal Welfare and the Environment

Naruto et al. vs David Slater

David Slater is a wildlife photographer who documents endangered species. His photographs have been published in books and licensed around the world. In 2011, he traveled to Indonesia and procured for sale photographs that were to become famous, both for the quality of the images and for the controversy they generated. It became a legal case because some of the photographs were not taken by Slater, but by an Indonesian native named Naruto.

As Naruto took the photograph, albeit using Slater's camera, the copyright in the photograph should belong to Naruto, right?

Except that Naruto is a macaque monkey, and there is no legal precedent for a non human animal owning intellectual property.

The legal action was brought on Naruto's behalf by People for the Ethical Treatment of Animals (PETA).

Should PETA, and Naruto, have won this case? Is there an ethical case to be made that Naruto, and not David Slater, owned the copyright to the photographs?

To answer this question fully, we need to explore why copyright and intellectual property exist at all.

The U.S. Constitution empowers Congress to:

To promote the Progress of Science and useful Arts, by securing for limited Times to Authors and Inventors the exclusive Right to their respective Writings and Discoveries.

In the United States—where the case of *Naruto et al. v David Slater* was brought—there is no need register a copyright, as is required with patents and trademarks. Copyright exists automatically for any original artistic work. A photographer chooses lighting, angles, and framing. These are artistic choices, so photography is included in copyright.

Did David Slater make artistic choices when Naruto took a photograph? Did Naruto?

Slater says he created the whole situation. He traveled to Indonesia, made friends with a group of monkeys, and left the camera knowing that they would be fascinated by it.

The monkeys were apparently intrigued by their reflection in the lens. They would then press the button on the camera while looking directly into the lens. These *selfies* showed macaque monkeys very intimately, as they were staring directly at the lens when they took the picture.

Slater said he planned this. Naruto has said nothing.

But, does it seem probable that Naruto knew that hitting the button would take a photograph? Without that knowledge, how can anything Naruto did be considered an *artistic choice?* Artistic intent requires intent.

Ultimately, PETA tried to withdraw the case, having made a settlement with Slater. The Ninth Circuit Court of Appeals refused to allow this, but found against Naruto[1]

In American law, at least, non-human animals do not have the right to own property. If you wish to leave all your material goods to your cat, you need to set up a trust dedicated to the cat and leave the property to the trust. A corporate person is a person in American law, but a macaque monkey is not, and neither is a cat. You could, incidentally, use the same ploy of establishing a trust to leave your estate to your teddy bear.

Legal systems have made no determination on whether or not a visiting extra terrestrial is a person or whether artificial intelligence can be one. These issues may arise in the future. For now, we have quite enough controversies with corporate persons, chimpanzees, fetuses, and humans in a persistent vegetative state. There are different views on all of these questions, so it is worth pausing for a moment to consider some of them.

---

[1] https://cdn.ca9.uscourts.gov/datastore/opinions/2018/04/23/16-15469.pdf

The Genetic Criterion

Theologian and judge John Noonan argues[2] that:

A being with a human genetic code is a man.

He uses this to justify the notion that life begins at conception. The problem with this argument is that conception is not the start of human genetic code. The sperm and an ovum have human DNA *before* conception. Is every menstruation a miscarriage? Does every teenage boy commit genocide on a regular basis? Human DNA not only exists in someone in a persistent vegetative state, but also in a corpse that has been buried for months. It is not just in your reproductive cells, but in your dandruff. Does dandruff have rights too? Surely something more than human DNA is required?

The Cognitive Criteria

Mary Anne Warren sets out[3] a more complex set of criteria involving

1. Consciousness
2. Reasoning
3. Self-motivated activity
4. The capacity to communicate
5. Self-awareness
6. Moral agency

Collectively, these are considered the *cognitive criteria*. As with Noonan, Warren was participating in the debate about abortion. Her criteria exclude fetuses, but also exclude children below about 18 months and some learning-disabled people.

---

[2] John T.N., Jr. ed. 1970. *The Morality of Abortion: Legal and Historical Perspectives.* Cambridge, MA: Harvard University Press.
[3] Warren, M.A. 1973. "On the Moral and Legal Status of Abortion." *The Monist* 57 no. 1, pp. 43–61.

The Social Criterion

Others have suggested a *social criterion:* if society values you as a person, then you are a person. Your personhood hangs on whether or not someone cares about you. This is certainly how societies have behaved in the past, expanding their notions of personhood to include, for example, other races. It allows us to expand our definition further. Future generations may decide that other apes should be considered persons in law. But if the social criterion is the right definition, then the U.S. Supreme Court was arguably right when it decided the Dred Scott case and declared that black people, whether free or slaves, were inherently incapable of being considered U.S. citizens. The case was correctly decided according to the social criteria of the day. Does that sound right?

What if someone lives a solitary life and has no friends? What if no one cares about that someone? Is that someone therefore not a person? And, how many people need to value you. *Some* white Americans cared about black Americans when the Dred Scott case was decided. Some people today believe that our fellow primates should be accorded rights.

It also opens a fairly clear case of circular reasoning. Let us look at Dred Scott again. If the court reasoned that black people were not *persons* in the eyes of the law because no *persons* cared about them, then it needed a prior definition of *persons* to derive its definition. It is reasonable to assume that, even if only a minority of white people cared about black people, almost all black people did. The reasoning is, therefore, circular: if you exclude black people in your analysis, you also exclude them from your conclusion, and circular reasoning can never be logical.

The Sentience Criterion

Peter Singer has argued[4] that, while a fetus is not a person and a human being in a persistent vegetative state is not a person, animals with a developed central nervous system are. He is looking here at the *sentience* criterion: whether a being can experience pain and pleasure. He is consciously

---

[4] Singer, P. 1975. *Animal Liberation: A New Ethics for Our Treatment of Animals.* New York, NY: Random House.

following Jeremy Bentham's utilitarianism (see Chapter 1), but expanding the range of beings, we consider when thinking about the greatest good for the greatest number. Bentham himself toyed with the same thought: "The question is not 'Can they reason?', nor, 'Can they talk?', but 'Can they suffer?'"[5]

Most people in most countries eat meat. Very few humans practice cannibalism or have any desire to do so. This should make it clear that a large majority of people distinguish strongly between humans and other animals in making their ethical judgments, at least about food. The percentage of vegetarians in the population of western countries seems to be rising. While polling on the issue is inconsistent, and people will sometimes claim to be *vegetarian*, while not actually following a vegetarian diet, many western countries now seem to have significant vegetarian and vegan minorities. Polling suggests that 5–8 percent of the Americans identify as vegetarian, with slightly higher figures in the United Kingdom and Australia. But, these numbers are dwarfed in percentage terms, and most especially in absolute terms, by India. Some 31 percent of the population in India self-identifies as vegetarian. That amounts to 375 million people, more than the *entire* population of the United States.

In law, an animal is simply property, but it is property that has different protections. If you own a table, you can break the table's legs just because you enjoy the sound of hearing them snap. Most jurisdictions do not allow pet owners to do the same to a dog. Laws in the ante bellum Southern United States provided protections to slaves that did not apply to other property.

Is it ethical to wear fur?
How about leather?
How about silk?

The three Abrahamic faiths have a tradition of human mastery over the environment and over other animals. This stems from the genesis

---

[5] Bentham, J. 1780. *An Introduction to the Principles of Morals and Legislation.* London: T. Payne and son.

creation account in which God grants mastery over other living things to Adam.

There are, of course, different ways of interpreting this. Some thinkers stress a duty of stewardship, rather than the idea that nature exists for humans to exploit. This is the same tension as Kant set out in his concept of a human struggle between duty and pleasure.

Business struggles with the same tension and, of course, business-owners have the same wide range of opinions. But, businesses are also driven by the *invisible hand.* People want energy services, and so businesses find ways of meeting that demand. Some people simply want cheap energy and, in places where coal is plentiful and accessible, it can be cheap. Other businesses see opportunities in developing new technologies that will change energy production permanently.

Elon Musk correctly spotted that one barrier that prevents some people from adopting solar power is that solar panels tend to be ugly. He has invested in more efficient solar panels and improved methods of storing electricity—because people want electricity when the Sun is not shining—but also in more attractive looking solar panels.

Musk practices *purpose-driven capitalism,* but it is not a purely philanthropic effort. Let us suppose there is a significant breakthrough in the efficiency of solar panels to the point where everyone wants to install them. Even if that research comes from, say, a university project and is licensed to all manufacturers, if SolarCity (Musk's business) is the only company producing attractive panels, it could gain a significant market advantage.

He hopes to make a lot of money on this project. Does it matter if his motive is financial, environmental, or a combination of the two?

The Silicon Valley billionaires are driven by a number of passions, and they are investing big money in them. While they are individuals with different views, one theme is that climate change is a serious problem, and it is one that technology will solve.

The Princes of the Digital Age, and Why Their Passions Matter

- PayPal—Elon Musk, Max Levchin, Peter Thiel
- Facebook—Mark Zuckerberg, Peter Thiel
- Amazon—Jeff Bezos
- Google—Sergey Brin, Larry Page, Jeff Bezos

The passions of these people are important, because they have billions to spend on them

PayPal

PayPal partly grew out of *Stanford Review*—conservative/libertarian paper founded by Thiel and friends. The business then provided seed corn for many other ventures, including Facebook. Critics speak of the *PayPal mafia: avaricious capitalist, global manipulation* (Tom Hodgkinson, *Guardian*, 2008).[6]

Peter Thiel

- Philanthropy

Machine Intelligence Research Institute
OpenAI
Anti-aging research
Seasteading
Committee to Protect Journalists
Human Rights Foundation
Oslo Freedom Forum

Elon Musk

- Activities

SpaceX
Tesla Motors
SolarCity
Hyperloop
OpenAI

---

[6] https://theguardian.com/technology/2008/jan/14/facebook

Thiel and Musk also have been outspoken on political issues. Thiel has often been described as *neoconservative*. Musk calls himself *nationalist* and *nauseatingly pro-American* and donates to Democrats and Republicans. Thiel was an early and continuing supporter of Donald Trump.

There are themes to be found in their business investments and philanthropy, too, that may reflect conservative and libertarian views. For example, their business investments involve businesses moving into areas that governments have traditionally dominated, such as issuing currency and investing in infrastructure for transport, including space. Their investments also show a belief that climate change is real, but that business and technology, not politics and campaigning, provide solutions to the problem.

There is a theme that human lifespan can be extended, and we can colonize other worlds.

Their influences include the libertarian or objectivist thinker, Ayn Rand, who was also a science fiction (SF) novelist, and the SF novelist, Robert Heinlein, who was also something of a libertarian philosopher.

Jeff Bezos is the founder of Amazon and an early investor in Google. In March 2018, *Forbes* ranked him as the first centi-billionaire, when his wealth was measured at 112 billion U.S. dollars. By July of the same year, his wealth topped 150 billion U.S. dollars.

In addition to his holdings in Amazon and Google, he is the founder of space exploration and tourism company, Blue Origin, and the owner of the *Washington Post*.

Sergey Brin and Larry Page of Google have invested heavily in alternative energy through Google's philanthropic arm and are investors in Musk's Tesla Motors. Page has also supported the Singularity Institute, a transhumanist thinktank.

Again, we see similar themes, partly influenced by the conservative and libertarian views of the entrepreneurs. Many in Silicon Valley have donated heavily to Democrats, perhaps influenced by social issues. As a generalization, science seems to be a bigger theme for the Silicon Valley billionaires than is religion.

There are, of course, several public policy approaches to dealing with environmental problems. Most of these are designed to alter market behavior: either of businesses or consumers or both.

To an economist, an environmental problem is an example of an *externality*. This means that it is a cost that is not included in the price—it is external to the price.

Let us suppose that I mine coal and sell it to you so that you can heat your home. I need to buy the land, buy equipment, hire miners, and do many other things. These are costs that I absorb, so the price I charge to you needs to cover all these costs, and more, if I am to make money. You pay my price only if the value of the coal to you exceeds the cost. If you live in a cold climate and have no ready access to an alternative heating source, then you will probably benefit from paying my price, and we are both better off from the transaction.

But, when you burn the coal, smoke goes into the atmosphere. Particulates can trigger asthma in people nearby. Nitrous oxides and sulfur oxides can cause acid rain. Carbon dioxide contributes to climate change. These costs did not fall specifically on either of us, so they were not accounted for in the price you paid. These are external costs that fall either specifically on a third party or are so widely dispersed that although they do accrue in part to you and to me, our share of those costs is negligible.

The value of the coal, to you, exceeds the costs, to you. But, the total costs, including those borne by other people, may be higher.

And, some of these costs may not be borne by people at all. Some pollution involves damage to the open oceans. If you damage my lake or my river, I can sue you. But no one owns the oceans, so no one has standing to sue. As we saw at the beginning of the chapter, non-human animals—even our fellow primates—have no standing to sue in court: let alone plants or the oceans themselves.

One way of ensuring that these costs are properly accounted is to ensure that, as far as possible, natural resources are owned by someone. This was the case put by the economist Ronald Coase.[7] If you pollute my river, I can sue you for the damage. If you want permission to pollute my

---

[7] Coase, R .October 1960. "The Problem of Social Cost." *Journal of Law and Economics*, Vol 3, 1–44. The University of Chicago Press.

river, then you need to pay me a sufficient fee. If the fish are killed, then I can no longer fish in the river or charge anglers for the right to do so.

If you are polluting my river because you are a farmer and the run-off from your fields kills my fish, then we need to account for the full social cost of this. If your farm is feeding thousands of people and there were only ever six anglers who liked to fish in my river, then the social cost is low. You will easily be able to pay my fee for polluting my river.

Another possibility is that the government can impose taxes on you to cover the social cost of your pollution. This idea came from another economist, Arthur Pigou.[8] This might be more appropriate if the pollution you cause is more widespread, for example, affecting the atmosphere rather than a specific river that I own.

The biggest public policy debate around Pigou's ideas is the idea that countries—industrialized countries in particular—should adopt a carbon tax. In the United States, this has been supported by such luminaries as James Baker and George Schultz, both of whom had served as both Secretary of State and as Secretary of the Treasury in Republican administrations.[9]

Do nonhuman animals have rights? Does the environment itself have rights? Or, is this better expressed as the duties that we, as sentient, thinking animals have to other species and the environment as a whole?

Practical Exercise

Debate the motion:
This house believes that human rights should be extended to our fellow primates.
Note, this motion speaks of human rights, not civic rights such as voting and serving on juries. Your first role is to define what human rights are.

---

[8] Pigou, A.C. 1920. *The Economics of Welfare*. London: Macmillan.
[9] https://fortune.com/2018/09/10/baker-shultz-climate-plan/

Academic Exercise

Write an essay on the following topic:

This country should adopt a carbon tax.

Consider arguments that tend to support the proposition and arguments that tend to refute the proposition and reach a reasoned conclusion.

Resources

Star Trek: Voyager 2001. Author, Author. Season 7, Episode 20.

Wise, S. 2015. *Chimps have Feelings and Thoughts. They Should also have Rights*, TED.

CHAPTER 8

Compliance and the Culture of Ethics

Compliance is a big deal, and large companies have whole departments that are dedicated to it. The point is to make sure that the organization complies with all the relevant laws and rules.

The International Compliance Association defines[1] two levels of compliance:

> *Level 1 - compliance with the external rules that are imposed upon an organisation as a whole.*
> *Level 2 - compliance with internal systems of control that are imposed to achieve compliance with the externally imposed rules.*

This is complex, because laws apply to a particular legal jurisdiction—a country or state—and these may differ from one jurisdiction to another. There may also be rules that are set by non-governmental bodies. The New York Stock Exchange (NYSE), for example, has its own rules. Its rules are, of course, subject to the laws of the United States and of New York State, but companies that wish to be floated on NYSE need to obey NYSE's rules. Furthermore, NYSE's rules are implemented by the Securities and Exchange Commission (SEC), a statutory body.

Other stock exchanges have their own rules, which, of course, differ. It is one of the ways in which stock exchanges compete with each other for business. Some global companies have listings on multiple stock exchanges. Royal Dutch Shell, for example, has a primary listing on the London Stock Exchange and very significant secondary listings

---

[1] https://int-comp.org/careers/a-career-in-compliance/what-is-compliance/ (accessed September 11, 2019).

in Amsterdam and New York. When this author worked at Shell in the 1990s, it was one of only a small number of companies listed in London that announced quarterly, rather than half-yearly, financial results, as this was a requirement in New York, where some 30 percent of the group's shares were traded.

Professions—for example, lawyers and accountants—are often self-regulating. There will be rules set by the various professional societies or institutes. These may vary both by jurisdiction and by the qualification that the professional has. The British Isles, for example, have six competing institutes for chartered accountants. All of these bodies also train and qualify accountants around the world, as British qualifications have a cachet that qualifications from some other countries do not have. China is a big market for British professional qualifications.

The more complex compliance gets, the more it can end up being embedded in the culture of an organization. If people require constant training in the rules, this can end up with people focusing on the rules, instead of on any enduring principles as to right and wrong. This is likely to be a particular risk when managers in transnational corporations move from one market to another and have to learn a different set of rules for each jurisdiction. That process seems likely to promote a rules-based culture, rather than an ethics-based culture.

Let us consider, here, the question of avoiding discrimination in hiring decisions. If the hiring manager's first question is "How can we comply with the law?", rather than "How can we be both effective and fair?," the organization may end up losing something.

Regulations, themselves, can be very rules-based or very principles-based. This is true of laws, and of rules set by professional societies and institutes. This division goes back, at least, to the global divide between legal jurisdictions based on English Common Law and those based on Roman (or Napoleonic) Civil Law. Much of Europe uses Civil Law. Many countries in the Commonwealth of Nations use Common Law. The United States and 49 of its constituent states use Common Law. Louisiana uses Civil Law. The British Isles are also divided. Ireland uses Common Law, together with England and Wales, but Scotland uses Civil Law.

Civil Law is a rules-based system. Laws are extremely detailed and seek to anticipate every scenario. Necessarily, they leave loopholes because it is not possible to anticipate everything. Common Law is more princi-ples-based and creates broad duties for people, and businesses, to follow. These are fleshed out by precedents in court. This leaves fewer loopholes, but more gray areas, where the law is not clear, or, not clear yet, since there is no precedent.

An example of the difference between Common and Civil legal systems arose in the 1990s when it suddenly became possible for most people and most businesses to trade on digital platforms. In Germany, there was a great rush to enact a new law to *legalize* digital commerce. Existing law did not say it was permissible to enter into a contract on a digital platform, so the law needed to be amended. England's Common Law did not require any such amendment. (Though it got some anyway, via the European Union.) In English law, a contract is an agreement involving offer, acceptance, consideration, and intention to be legally bound. It can be oral, written, or digital. It does not matter if the offer and acceptance are communicated by post, phone, text, semaphore, or carrier pigeon.

A compliance culture can lead to people and organizations seeking to follow a particular formula to stay just inside the law. So, while compli-ance is important, it probably needs to be accompanied by ethics training to encourage people to look at problems in the light of broader, enduring, principles as well as a narrow reading of the law. It is, again, Peach's[2] point about obeying the spirit of the law as well as its plain text.

Compliance focuses not only on external rules such as laws, stock exchange requirements, and professional codes of ethics, but also the internal rules that an organization develops for itself. A business that has a robust policy of corporate social responsibility (CSR; see Chapter 5), for example, needs to ensure that there is compliance with the policy throughout the business and, as far as possible, throughout its supply chain. There seems little point in deciding that you will minimize your direct climate footprint if you then outsource key elements of the business to a supplier that does not have the same policy.

---

[2] Peach, L. 1987. "Corporate Responsibility." In *Effective Corporate Relations* ed. Hart, N. Maidenhead: McGraw Hill

---

Patagonia's Fourfold Screening

Outdoor clothing supplier, Patagonia[3] has a policy of *fourfold screening* in choosing suppliers. The four elements for which potential suppliers are screened are:

1. Sourcing: price, capacity, delivery.
2. Quality: garment quality up to standard.
3. Social responsibility.
4. Environmental responsibility.

All four areas have equal veto powers, so managers responsible for social and environmental responsibility can veto a supplier arrangement, no matter how good the supplier is on the other elements.

But, such compliance policies require auditing. Patagonia is signed up to the Fair Labor Association's (FLA's) code on social and environmental responsibility that has, itself, been criticized by some groups. Patagonia, therefore, not only audits its supply chain, but shares the results of its audits with other FLA members. This ensures wider transparency and saves the factories from *audit fatigue*.

Critics such as United Students Against Sweatshops has claimed the FLA's code is too weak and the auditing should be more independent, for example, by universities.

Policies prioritizing *fair trade* can be a key part of compliance within the supply chain, but can be taken too far. Production in developing countries is often cheaper than in western countries. People are paid less. They are also sometimes less well educated and less productive. If factories in developing countries were not cheaper, they would not win very much business. They are required to compete on price.

Campaigns to persuade western retailers to boycott cheap labor in developing countries can, therefore, have the effect of forcing them to boycott *all* labor in developing countries, bringing the whole process of

---

[3] https://youtu.be/aS72nt-BhQA (accessed September 11, 2019).

developing to a stop. Being employed in a factory you or I might label a *sweatshop* might still be better than being unemployed.

This may not even be an accidental by product of the campaigns. Labor unions in the west exist to protect the interests of their own members, potentially even it is at the expense of poorer people elsewhere in the world. Calls for protectionism have been growing in western countries in recent years, with candidates such as Bernie Sanders and Donald Trump putting them at the heart of their presidential campaigns.

Both governmental and non governmental organizations certify some consumer claims. For example, the claim that foodstuffs are *organic* requires compliance with very specific rules. In the United States, compliance is managed by the U.S. Department of Agriculture (USDA) and in the United Kingdom by a charity, the Soil Association.

Other terms, such as *vegetarian* and *vegan*, may seem more straightforward, but also need defining and monitoring. In the United Kingdom, the Vegetarian Society's green "V" logo is often used on menus and food packaging to show compliance with the Society's definition of *vegetarian*. Still, in the realm of foodstuffs, the terms *kosher* and *halal* are religiously defined, and it will typically be, at least, a breach of contract and usually a criminal offense to claim compliance with these rules while not actually abiding by them.

In finance, Sharia (Islamic law) requires similar levels of compliance with religious codes and for a bank to claim that a specific financial product is Sharia-compliant without following the appropriate rules would normally be fraud.

All of this means that even Level 1 compliance can be broken down into several distinct sublevels:

(a) Compliance with legal requirements.
(b) Compliance with the requirements of external voluntary organizations with regard to internal management—for example, stock exchange rules.
(c) Compliance with the requirements of external voluntary organizations with regard to product claims, such as *organic* or *Sharia*.

While Sublevels (b) and (c) are not generally applicable rules, they may nonetheless be legal issues, as claiming to comply with the rules, while not actually doing so can be fraudulent.

Is It Kosher?

Let us suppose you are organizing a wedding in Brooklyn, New York. You know that some of guests at the wedding will be Jewish, so you approach a caterer that advertises that it can cater for kosher events. You agree a contract that specifies the number of guests, the price per guest, and the fact that all the food must be kosher.

On the day, however, the caterer provides a shellfish-based first course and bacon double cheeseburgers as the main course. Your guests are extremely unhappy.

Naturally, you ask for your money back. The caterer refuses. Shellfish, bacon, and mixing meat and dairy are all perfectly permissible in kosher rules, the caterer insists.

So, naturally you decide to sue the caterer. You offer to produce any number of rabbis in court who will testify that the caterer's interpretation of the word *kosher* is peculiar to the point of being unique. You approach the firm of Cohen and Weinberg to represent you.

Are you likely to prevail in court?

The perhaps surprising answer is that you might very well lose. American courts are very reluctant to define or enforce religious rules, even as part of a contract, under the First Amendment's bar on establishing religion.[4] A similar contractual clause that required food to be vegetarian would be enforceable.

State laws that define as fraud any false claim to be *kosher* or *halal* have hit similar hurdles. You would be best off writing into the contract the specific rules that you require the contractor to follow.

---

[4] https://4dca.org/Opinions/Opinions-Archive?qf=&sort=attr_disposition_date_dt%20desc,%20attr_case_number_s%20ascandview=embed_customandsearchtype=opinionsandlimit=20andstartdate=andenddate=anddate[year]=anddate[month]=anddate[day]=andquery=andoffset=0(accessed September 11, 2019).

The approach by American courts is surprising, because contract law has traditionally been based on the concept of *meeting of minds*. If both parties have an agreement between them and the action required is not itself not illegal, a contractual term will normally be enforceable, if there is a generally understood meaning of the words involved. (If your particular synagogue operated an unusually strict definition of *kosher*, you probably could not reasonably expect the caterer to know that, unless you specified it in the contract.)

You could, of course, approach a Beth Din—a Jewish religious court. If the caterer agreed to private arbitration by a Beth Din, you would be likely to win your case, and, of course, rabbis would be free to tell their community that the caterer did not comply with kosher rules, and Jewish people should, therefore, avoid that particular business.

A Beth Din, Sharia court, or ruling of any other voluntary organization is a form of private arbitration. They can only be binding if both sides agree to be bound by the ruling. Effectively, they have the same legal status as "Judge Judy," the CBS TV show.

There is, at least arguably, a third level of compliance not covered by the definition of the International Compliance Association.

Level 3: Compliance with Other Aspects of the Organization's Own Policies

While organizations certainly have internal policies that are designed to comply with externally established standards, they will also frequently have policies that exist for another reason. Patagonia's fourfold screening (see aforementioned) is a policy aimed principally at ensuring the group's own values, although compliance with the FLA's standards also informs the policies. Setting out internal policies that go beyond those required of competitors can be a key competitive differentiator. Auditing the business's internal procedures and those of businesses in the supply chain is another key aspect of a robust compliance policy.

Compliance in the Age of Cultural Clashes

Both Jewish and Islamic religious rules require that animals being slaughtered for food should be killed according to specific requirements. In particular, they require that the animal should be killed by a single cut to the throat. This probably seemed like the most humane method at the time that the rules were written, but modern methods of slaughter usually require that the animal is stunned by a bolt to the head before being cut. Both Jewish and Islamic authorities are divided on the question of whether rules permit pre-stunning of the animals.

Both as a matter of public law and for the internal compliance purposes of individual businesses, this issue creates deep conflict between animal welfare activists and religious liberty lobbyists. Some countries, such as the United States, have specific protections for religious liberty that might prevent some types of regulation of animal slaughter. The United States has no rules requiring pre-stunning, though this is the normal practice in most modern slaughter houses, other than those set up to serve particular religious communities.

These debates create conflicts within Jewish and Islamic communities, as well as between members of the faiths and animal welfare activists.

The Mufti of Delhi declared in a 1935 fatwa that the act of stunning, since it does not actually kill the animal, is permitted before the cut.

Rabbi Norman Solomon has claimed (2000) that, to many Reform Jews, ethical considerations take precedence over Jewish dietary requirements and choose not to eat kosher meat at all.

In Europe, only one country (Slovenia) bans ritual slaughter altogether. Several countries, including Denmark, Norway, and Sweden, require that animals be stunned before the cut. Several, including Estonia, Greece, and Austria, require post-cut stunning. Finland requires stunning simultaneous with the cut.

Should the ritual slaughter of animals be restricted? Or banned?

Under the Religious Freedom Restoration Act, the United States federal government "shall not substantially burden a person's exercise of religion even if the burden results from a rule of general applicability". A number of U.S. states have adopted similar rules.

There are two conditions under which such burdens are permitted:

1. The"burden" must be necessary to further some compelling government interest.
2. The rule must be the least burdensome way to further that interest.

Would a restriction on religious slaughter meet these tests?

Would such a rule be a "substantial burden"? It creates no necessary conflict between public law and religious rules. Neither Judaism nor Islam requires adherents to eat meat. Adherents could comply with both public law and religious rules by becoming vegetarian.

Is protecting animal welfare a "compelling government interest"?

What would be the"least burdensome" way to further that interest?

The Author's Dilemma

In which chapter should this discussion be included? Including it under *Animal Welfare and Environmental Protection* would have created a particular context for considering these issues. Including it under *Harassment, Discrimination, and Inclusion* would have created a different context. Is including it in the more neutral context of compliance a reasonable compromise?

Triple Bottom Line Reporting

Many organizations now operate some form of *triple bottom line* (TBL or 3BL) reporting. This takes the traditional concept of the financial bottom line and applies it to reporting environmental and social impacts. Financial, environmental, and social factors are often referred to as *profit, planet and people,* so the term PPP reporting is also used for some social audits.

By taking this approach, organizations (including, but not limited to, businesses) are acknowledging the idea that businesses have wider responsibilities than to shareholders, arguably departing from Friedman's widely quoted, and widely criticized, *New York Times* essay (see Chapter 1).

There is no necessary conflict between the three bottom lines, however. Businesses that audit their impact on social and environmental issues can still be profitable. Potentially, if customers and staff seek out such businesses and are more loyal to them because of shared values, such businesses can be more profitable.

Howard Schultz of Starbucks did not ask shareholders to accept a lower return in exchange for the good feeling of supporting marriage equality. He politely suggested to shareholders who disagree with his stance that if they think they can get a better return than 38 percent they could invest elsewhere.[5]

In the case of preserving people and the planet, there is no necessary conflict between Kant's principles of pleasure and duty.

But, what if there is? Do shareholders actually care about the environment or fairtrade issues?

Plainly, there is one aspect of sustainability that is of key relevance to shareholders: the ability to sustain profits. Despite the claim by media commentators that the stock exchange only cares about short-term profits, a business that was neglecting its own infrastructure to report immediate profits would struggle to find investors. The biggest investment funds are pension funds, which wish to see a return over many decades in order to meet their financial obligations.

But, financial sustainability is only one aspect. As we have already explored in Chapters 5 (CSR) and 7 (Animal Welfare and the Environment), some costs to the world as a whole do not feature in pricing. Damage to the wider environment is not costed unless the owner of the property in question can, and is likely to, sue the polluter. No one has standing to sue on behalf of unowned property, such as the seas or the atmosphere, and nonhuman animals have no standing to sue.

If we as potential customers, employees, and investors wish to boycott businesses that harm the environment, we can only do so if we have the information.

---

[5] https://youtu.be/oAb7rZ1y60Q (accessed January 23, 2020).

Some investment funds absolutely do wish to make responsible behavior a condition of investment. Investors are, after all, people. Like customers and staff, they have a wide range of views on ethical, social, and political questions. But, the ultimate beneficiaries of these investments—people saving for a pension, for example—are several stages removed from the process of monitoring. They delegate the investment decisions to professional fund managers who, in turn, delegate running the businesses to boards of directors.

Unless you have specified that you want such ethical criteria included in the investment decisions, then fund managers have a fiduciary duty to invest for the best return.

And, the individual beneficiaries might not, in any case, be choosing the pension fund. It may be linked to an employer. The layers of accountability are complex, and it is likely that most savers have little or no idea what ethical decisions are being made on their behalf.

Greater transparency about how businesses are run is therefore likely to be valuable, but despite the several decades that have elapsed since John Elkington conceived the term,[6] *Triple Bottom Line* is still rather vaguely defined.

Reporting the financial bottom line has clear and well-established standards. More detail is typically required of larger and publicly traded companies, but the basic processes of creating a balance sheet are widely understood.

Social and environmental issues are harder to define, measure, and cost. Some costs may emerge only years later. Some problems we presently regard as insoluble may be soluble by future generations.

Social and environmental auditing is also not compulsory. Businesses do not have to report on these issues. While "The Shell Report", an independently audited report of the group's triple bottom line, was first published just a few years after Elkington conceived the phrase, there is still neither an industry standard for reporting nor a universal expectation that such reporting is expected.

---

[6] Elkington, J. 1994. "Toward the Sustainable Corporation: Win-Win-Win Business Strategies for Sustainable Development." *California Management Review* 36, no. 2, pp. 90–100.

Could governments or stock exchanges make TBL reporting compulsory? Sure. They *could*. But, they would have to arrive at a clear definition of the term first.

Practical Exercise

Develop a case for your CEO arguing that, in addition to compliance training, the business should adopt ethics training for all staff.
Write a two-page persuasive memo.

Academic Exercise

Write an essay on the following topic:
Common Law is to be Preferred to Civil Law or Sharia Law
Present arguments that tend to support the proposition and arguments that tend to refute the proposition and reach a reasoned conclusion.

Resources

International Compliance Association: https://int-comp.org/
International Compliance Professionals Association: https://icpainc.org/
The Audiopedia, *What is Triple Bottom Line?* https://youtu.be/2xgIVJU5PWQ
Tutor2u *Corporate Social Responsibility—Elkington's Triple Bottom Line* https://youtu.be/x9WvCJ3oOL0
Murphy, Christopher, *What is a Social Audit* https://investopedia.com/terms/s/social-audit.asp

CHAPTER 9

Public Safety

That products should be safe to use is, of course, a major concern for customers. It is also a major issue for shareholders, as an unsafe product might attract law suits. It may well be a concern for employees, as there could be dangers in the manufacturing process too.

But, such general truisms do not capture the whole story.

Products may have dangers that are hard to detect or cannot be proved. They may pose dangers to people other than the customers, whose standing to sue may be doubtful. They may pose dangers to people who are vulnerable. They may even pose dangers that are well known, and that the customer voluntarily accepts.

We also need to account for social trends. Safety—or, at least, an ever-rising standard of safety—is a luxury. People in wealthier countries are happy to pay for higher safety standards. This is much less the case with poorer people. In recent years, western countries have seen increasing standards of safety accompanied by increasing fears. Some have been critical of this trend with Lukianoff and Haidt,[1] describing it as a culture of *safetyism* and others using the pejorative *snowflakes*.

An obvious example of increased safety would be in road traffic accidents. The raw number of accidents, including fatal accidents, is governed by several trends, including the safety of the vehicles, safety of the driving, and distances traveled. The numbers of fatalities per vehicle and per passenger distance traveled have been falling for decades. Many countries, however, have seen greater population, more vehicles on the road, and more people traveling greater distances. Nonetheless, the overall trend of fatalities has been down in recent years; by 2007–2008, figures for the United States had already fallen below those of 1961.

---

[1] Lukianoff, G. and Haidt, J. 2018. *The Coddling of the American Mind.* New York, NY: Penguin Books.

Vehicles are now generally fitted with more safety systems to prevent accidents and with products and systems to protect occupants in the event of an accident. In the past decades, many cars did not even contain seatbelts. This is now universal, except in classic cars that are still on the road. In the United States, 49 states—New Hampshire is the exception—make wearing a seatbelt compulsory. There are other countries where this is not the case. Some years ago, the author lived for a while in Tbilisi, in the Republic of Georgia. Wearing seatbelts was not only not compulsory or socially expected, drivers would often tie up their seatbelts so that passengers could not use them. They interpreted wearing a seatbelt as an insult to their driving skills.

It is likely that people are better drivers, too, with increasing awareness of the risks associated with driving while intoxicated.

Despite falling fatality rates, the United States has higher driving fatalities than do countries in Western Europe. How much higher depends on how you measure them. Fatalities per head of population are around three times as high as European countries. But, Americans have more cars, so, perhaps, that is to be expected. Fatalities per vehicle are closer to twice as high. But, Americans drive further so, again, that is to be expected. Fatalities per billion passenger kilometers (the international standard measure for transport safety) are about 50 percent higher, and this may be linked to higher speeds, especially in urban areas and a higher permitted blood-alcohol level.[2]

So, how dangerous is driving? In the United States, there are 7.1 fatalities per billion passenger kilometers. At a highway driving speed of 100 kmh (a little over 66 mph), that is 10 million hours of driving or one fatality per 1,408,451 hours. That is over 58,000 days or 160 years. On average, you can expect to die or kill after 160 years or so of constant driving—assuming you have not died of something else first.

---

[2] Luoma, J. and Sivak, M. January, 2013. "Why is Road Safety in the U.S. not on Par with Sweden, the U.K., and the Netherlands? Lessons to be Learned." *University of Michigan Transportation Research Institute.*

Tullock's Spike

Let us suppose that you are planning to go out drinking and considering whether to drive or take a taxi. If you approach the decision rationally, you will consider the physical risks you will face by driving home drunk. But, your car has seatbelts and airbags. You have side impact protection. You have lane keeping assist. You can not only reduce the chance of a collision, but greatly reduce your chance of serious injury in the event of a collision. As a result, you decide to drive, and on the way home, you kill a cyclist.

Safety is not always good. Irresponsible driving's consequences *to the driver* are reduced. But, this may encourage that irresponsible behavior. It is what economists call *moral hazard*. The cost, to you, of drunk driving is lower, so, you are more likely to engage in the practice, and thus, endanger other people. That is the negative side of increased safety. That is why, the economist Gordon Tullock[3] suggested that maybe cars should have spikes installed on the steering wheel. By making driving more dangerous for the driver, it could make it safer for other, less protected, road users.

Higher-quality safety equipment in sport can have a similar effect. Boxing gloves reduce the risk of immediate injury to both parties— breaking bones in the hand and cutting the face. But, they create more powerful, but cushioned, blows. These create a rocking motion in the head that, over time, can cause brain injuries. Better protection for American football players can lead to them playing more aggressively and taking more risk than, say, rugby players. Again, this may contribute to long-term brain damage.

Since Tullock first suggested the spike as a thought experiment, in-car safety measures have developed further. This process is far from complete.

---

[3] Alex. 2017. "The Tullock Spike." *Weird Universe.* http://weirduniverse.net/blog/comments/tullock_spike (accessed September 9, 2019).

How will driverless cars deal with ethical decision making? What ethical code should guide a machine? Well, for the moment at least, that is simple. People will program the driverless cars. The cars will make the decisions that people want them to make.

So Bonnefon, Shariff, and Rahwan[4] set out to discover what people want. They created a dilemma based on the trolley problems we had discussed in Chapter 1. Should a driverless car swerve to avoid a group of pedestrians, even at the risk of killing the passenger in the car? They discovered that people strongly favored the Benthamite, utilitarian approach. The car should seek the greatest happiness—or least harm— to the greatest number. The problem is that people also said they would not buy a car like that. People would only buy a car that maximized the owner's safety. People want *everyone else* to buy cars that maximize societal safety, but they want to make a different choice themselves.

So, perhaps the solution is regulation. The problem here is that people say if such cars were the only autonomous vehicles available, they still would not buy them. They would continue to drive cars themselves, and not transition to the new, presumably safer, cars.

If driverless cars meet the standard of being 90 percent safer than drivers, should driving then be banned?

Driving is often set up as the standard against which safety of other products and, especially, transport options, can be measured. Most people drive frequently and everyone knows people who drive frequently. Obviously, most of those people are not killed. If you can establish that any given activity is safer than driving, then most people will conclude that it is tolerably safe. Driving has well-known dangers, but they are dangers that we willingly accept for the benefits that it brings.

Of course, people may underestimate their own personal risk from driving. The average may be one death per 160 years of driving, but individual risk is variable. People who drive drunk are at significantly more risk. And, not everyone, even when sober, has the same driving skill. Your

---

[4] Bonnefon, J. F., Shariff, A., and Rahwan, I. June, 2016. "The Social Dilemma of Autonomous Vehicles." *Science* 352, no. 6293, pp. 1573–1576.

own risk will be lower if you are a better than average driver. Some 90 percent of the people probably assess their own skills as better than average.

But, it would still be a good thing if driving were safer.

How Much Is a Life Worth?

Let us suppose that you are manufacturing a car. It has a safety bug. A rear end collision creates a measurable danger that the gas tank will blow up. You could install a plastic block. That would cost 13 U.S. dollars per car. Not installing it would cost 200 lives per year. Each of those lives would cost you 200,000 U.S. dollars in compensation. This means that installing the plastic block would cost you more than getting sued for 200 lives per year. (The prices, both for the plastic block and for a human life, are in 1970's dollars.)

So, you don't install the plastic block, right?

What if increasing the safety of the car cost more than 13 U.S. dollar per car? What if it was 10,000 U.S. dollars? Or 20,000 U.S. dollars? What if the safety measures put up the price of new cars so much that people postpone the purchase and keep driving their older, less-safe, cars for longer?

Shouldn't people be able to choose a cheaper, less-safe, car if they want to, provided it is made clear that it is slightly less safe?

There is a video widely available on YouTube (presently titled *Milton Friedman – Morality and Capitalism*) in which Nobel Prize-winning economist Milton Friedman tackles these issues in a question and answer session with students.

What about airlines? Should they be able to choose to buy less-safe planes? Is there a difference between an aircraft manufacturer quoting a standard price and then saying that some safety features are available at a premium price or quoting a completely *a la carte* price list? Or, agreeing to remove some features to save money at the airline's request?

In the context of buying airplanes, there may not be much difference. The price will have been negotiated over months or years, and both negotiating teams will be expert in the process and in safety issues. There is not the imbalance of power that exists between a motor manufacturer and many of *its* customers.

In 2019, *The Wall Street Journal*[5] reported that Boeing had not been transparent and had not told airlines or the Federal Aviation Authority that it had disabled some safety features on its 737 Max aircraft. The same features had been fully functional on previous versions of the product.

Can a Business Ethically Sell Tobacco?

Tobacco, like cars, has known and well-understood dangers. People buy the product knowing perfectly well that, in the long term, it is very damaging to the health. Smoking is strongly linked to both cancer and heart disease, which are the two most common causes of death in most developed countries. In the United States, for example, the Center for Disease Control reports[6] that heart disease causes 23.5 percent of deaths and cancer 21.3 percent. Of course, there are many other hereditary, lifestyle, and environmental factors linked to both heart disease and cancer, but smoking is a significant contributor. Today, tobacco companies—and governments—are very transparent about the risks. But, people typically take up smoking when they are young, and the risks seem very distant. Nicotine is addictive and hard to give up.

The risk with tobacco is cumulative. Driving is very different. A serious road traffic accident often kills people immediately. Younger drivers are at more risk than their more experienced colleagues. But, young smokers know that they are not in immediate danger. The risk is typically decades in the future.

Tobacco is an unusual product. Cars, guns, and all sorts of other things are dangerous if they are used badly. A car driven by a drunk or a gun wielded by a criminal can kill you. But, tobacco is dangerous if you use it exactly as you are supposed to use it. If you follow the manufacturer's

---

[5] Pazsztor, A. April, 2019. "Boeing Didn't Advise Airlines, FAA That It Shut Off Warning System." *Wall Street Journal.*

[6] Nichols, H. July, 2019. "What are the Leading Causes of Death in the US?" *Medical News Today.*

recommendations perfectly, it can still kill you, albeit probably many years in the future.

Tobacco manufacturers have been accused of marketing their products toward young people via the use of cartoon characters such as Joe Camel and using iconic images such as the Marlboro Man to promote the idea that tobacco is rugged and archetypically American. America is associated with modernity and aspiration in many developing countries. But, in America itself, tobacco sales have been declining for decades, precisely because the product causes systemic health issues that are the opposite of rugged independence.

To those of you who think it is not ethical to sell tobacco, is it ethical to sell alcohol? That has known risks too. It is also strongly linked to heart disease and to obesity, which, itself, is linked to heart disease.

Furthermore, alcohol changes people's behavior. Some people become violent when drunk. Almost everyone suffers from impaired reaction times, which is why drunk-driving is banned. Alcohol may not cause quite as much risk to the consumer as tobacco does, but it may cause *more* risk to third parties. It is one thing to say you are allowed to take risks with your own life, but risking other people's lives is a more serious matter.

Is it ethical to sell products that people may use to commit crimes? For example, should gun manufacturers be made liable for criminal and negligent use of their products? If so, are automakers liable for the larger number of deaths that their products cause, or do we assume that "cars don't kill people. People kill people?"

Cars, recreational drugs, and guns are all products that consumers fully understand are dangerous. What about vulnerable consumers?

Let us consider the question of people living in nursing homes.

The first issue we face in this issue is that there is frequently a difference between the customer and the consumer. The person living in the home is the consumer, but may not be the person paying the bills. That could be an insurance company. It could be an arm of the government, such as a state, a city, or the Veterans' Administration. It could be a relative of the consumer, either meeting the cost or acting with power of attorney over the consumer's affairs.

The nursing home resident may not be equipped to make the case for better treatment or even be fully aware that the customer service is inadequate. All of this applies to senior care, but also to homes for children and for vulnerable, but non-elderly, adults.

So, let us consider a case in which a nursing home is being negligent and its employees are abusing residents. There are many types of abuse, of course: neglect, sexual, physical, and emotional. Who even monitors whether this is happening? No system of control, whether it is lawsuits or oversight by an external regulator, can be effective if there is no one monitoring things. The resident is on the spot, but may not have the means to monitor the standard of care.

The person paying the bills may not be on the spot, and may—particularly in the case of a government or insurance company—have no particular motive to monitor the standard of care. That might end up increasing the costs.

This would be an example of Milton and Rose Friedman's four ways to spend money set out in their book "Free to Choose.".[7] This will be explored in more detail in Chapter 12, Government Ethics, but the Friedmans set out four spending scenarios

1. Spending your own money on yourself.
2. Spending another person's money on yourself.
3. Spending your own money on someone else.
4. Spending someone else's money on someone else.

Naturally, it is in the first scenario where people tend to be focused on both quality and value for money. The nursing home or care facility scenario will usually be an example of Case 3 or 4: a relative spending her or his own money (or money from an estate from which the relative will be a beneficiary) on a family member, or a government organization or insurer spending money on the consumer.

In this particular example of Case 3, the relative may well have a high level of concern for the consumer, although this is likely to be less so with the government.

---

[7] Friedman, M. and Friedman, R. 1990. *Free to Choose: A Personal Statement.* New York, NY, USA: Mariner Books. Originally published in 1980. The 1990 version is available with video chapters.

So, how can a level of care be established and monitored?

Is there a case for an independent certification agency that could audit homes and issue certificates as to their policies and implementation?

How should a business market safety? Let us suppose, in the future, one of the businesses marketing autonomous vehicles has a significantly better safety record than others. Should it use that as a product differentiator? At first glance, that would seem to be a good idea.

But, airlines never market on the basis of safety. There is a famous scene in the movie *Rain Man*, where Dustin Hoffman's character claims that Qantas is the only airline that has never had a fatal accident.

But, airlines almost never talk about safety. There is an urban legend that they all agreed not to, but it seems more probable that they simply do not want to talk about the issue because it makes people nervous. Judged by the standard transport sector metric of deaths per billion passenger kilometers, flying is vastly safer than any other form of transport. Walking is actually the second most dangerous, after motorcycles. But, some people have a paralyzing fear of flying, and many others are at least a bit nervous of it. In this context, it is not in the interests of airlines to talk about safety. Their ads never say, "Fly with us and we will try really hard to make sure the wings don't fall off when we are halfway across the Atlantic." They say "get on our plane, and when you get off, you will be in Paris, New York, or Tahiti."

At least to start off with, people will be similarly nervous of autonomous vehicles. People will expect clear evidence that autonomous vehicles are at least as safe—and preferably much safer—than drivers. Remember, merely being safer than average is not the point if the driver believes himself or herself to be a better than average driver.

Practical Exercise

The 18th Amendment to the U.S. Constitution was ratified in January 1919 and repealed, by the 21st Amendment in December 1933. It banned the manufacture, sale, or transportation of intoxicating liquors and followed decades of campaigning by the temperance movement. Prohibition is often referred to as *the noble experiment*. The dangers of alcohol are well known. The advantages if its consumption is curtailed are obvious. But, it is widely acknowledged that it did not work. People continued to consume alcohol, and organized crime was able to build huge fortunes, and to corrupt law enforcement via its monopoly on the supply of alcohol. Its power was dented by the repeal of prohibition.

Of course, organized crime still operates in the United States. It supplies other drugs, prostitution, gambling, and other services that customers are quite willing to purchase despite their prohibition.

In other countries, especially in the Muslim world, alcohol remains banned.

Laws that prohibit voluntary exchanges are inherently difficult to enforce without police resorting to entrapment, illegal searches, or other stretching of the rules of evidence, as the only witnesses are often both engaged in illegal behavior. There is no one to even report the crime, let alone testify.

Debate the motion: This house believes that it is time to end drug prohibition.

Another obvious alternative would be consider adding to the list of prohibited drugs. Perhaps, tobacco should be banned.

Academic Exercise

Critique the images promoted by tobacco companies, such as Joe Camel and the Marlboro Man. Is there evidence that they are effective in promoting misinformation about tobacco?

Resources

Last Week Tonight with John Oliver (HBO): Tobacco. https://youtu.be/6UsHHOCH4q8 (accessed October 19, 2019).

Last Week Tonight with John Oliver (HBO): Tobacco Update. https://youtu.be/EROql_0GgiQ (accessed October 19, 2019).

CHAPTER 10

The Ethics of Data Management

Data form the primary asset of the new economy. People are comparing big data companies, such as Google and Facebook, with the historic *seven sisters* of the oil industry. As data become easier to gather and manage, they also become more valuable.

Business is only beginning to explore ways of monetizing this asset. So far, the big one is advertising. By enabling advertisers to identify ever smaller target audiences, it can increase the value of advertising. Buying ads in huge media events, such as major sports competitions or the Oscars, is very expensive and, for most businesses, wasteful. Most of the people you reach will not be interested in your product. More precisely targeted ads can be much better value for money.

But, this is only the beginning, and we have not begun to imagine all the possible uses for these data. Google and Uber, for example, are at the forefront of developing autonomous (self-driving) vehicles. The data they are gathering about actual traffic conditions and actual driver behavior are critical to informing the driving algorithm.

The technical and commercial uses of data are at their very early stages. But, what are the ethics of data management?

This chapter considers three fundamental questions:

1. How data are gathered?
2. How data are used?
3. How data are secured?

Gathering Data

It is easy to say that, provided there is transparency, there should be no problems. Overwhelmingly—except when dealing with governments—people have voluntarily handed over their data. Typically, people agree to terms and conditions that involve sacrificing their rights to data in exchange for some valuable service. Provided that this full transparency exists, what is the problem? We all read those terms and conditions before we agree, don't we?

Consent is not always fully informed consent, and data is not always gathered with consent. Transparency can even be a self-defeating goal. Transparency is not served if you do not give enough detail about how you plan to use the data. But, it is also not served if you give so much detail that people tire of reading through it or find it hard to comprehend. It is not as if there is some middle ground either, as the right balance of disclosure will vary from one person to another.

Unlike a government, a private corporation cannot force you to hand over data. If it is to gather data lawfully, it must secure consent via some sort of *purchase*. Store loyalty cards are just such an arrangement. You agree to let the store have information about your shopping habits and your credit; in exchange, the store offers you discounts, early access to new lines, or some other benefit.

Data businesses such as Google and Facebook offer you a valuable service at no charge in exchange for access to your data. You agreed to this when you accepted the terms and conditions of service. At the smaller scale, enabling *cookies* on your Internet browser means you do not have to re-enter your password every time you visit a site. The site recognizes you, but it can also track your browsing history.

This may not bother you, but it is easy to imagine circumstances when it might. Let us suppose you are about to give a major business presentation and it involves showing a clip from YouTube. Recognizing you as a regular user, YouTube has suggestions for you based on your past browsing behavior. As a result, your boss, colleagues, and clients, get to see what the YouTube algorithm predicts will be interesting videos for you. It is easy to see how this might be embarrassing to someone who has been viewing videos about a personal health problem. Displaying a screen to your colleagues that shows pornographic material may be more than embarrassing; it could be career-limiting.

Not all data is gathered lawfully. For example, Google revealed in 2010 that it had inadvertently been gathering data from home Wi-Fi networks via its Google Streetview car.[1] The intention had been not to gather *payload data,* but it turned out that such data was being gathered.

In the United States, the FBI and the office of Immigration and Customs Enforcement (ICE) have been using data from state departments of motor vehicles (DMVs) as an images database. People give their state DMV a photograph for their drivers' licenses. This may not be, strictly, unlawful, but seems not to have been authorized either by Congress or by state legislatures. In a federal country, founded on a system of individual rights, state governments have been sharing personal data with federal law enforcement agencies without any political or legal oversight. Individuals do not typically consent to such routine sharing when they apply for a driver's license.[2] So, who consented? No one.

But, even when data are gathered lawfully, there may less than full transparency. Consulting firm Deloitte[3] found that more than 90 percent of the users admit to not reading terms and conditions before agreeing that they accept them. This may be an underestimate. Research by Obar and Oeldorf-Hirsch[4] found 97 percent of people signing up for a spoof networking site agreed to terms and conditions that stated data would be shared with the National Security Agency (NSA) and users were required to give up their first-born children.

How much transparency is there when businesses are aware that people do not read, and may not be capable of comprehending, page after page of dense legal copy?

---

[1] https://theguardian.com/technology/2010/may/15/google-admits-storing-private-data (accessed September 18, 2019).

[2] https://washingtonpost.com/technology/2019/07/07/fbi-ice-find-state-drivers-license-photos-are-gold-mine-facial-recognition-searches/ (accessed September 18, 2019).

[3] https://businessinsider.com/deloitte-study-91-percent-agree-terms-of-service-without-reading-2017-11 (accessed September 18, 2019).

[4] https://papers.ssrn.com/sol3/papers.cfm?abstract_id=2757465 (accessed September 18, 2019).

It is fairly straightforward to gather data on social media sites by offering users the opportunity to play a game or participate in a quiz. In this instance, the organization is not offering a powerful search engine or a widely used social network in exchange for your data; it is simply offering to tell you what sort of potato you would be or which superhero you would date in the competing Marvel and DC universes. (This author was delighted to learn that he could date Black Widow in the Marvel universe and Wonder Woman in DC.)

It is quizzes of this type that were associated with the data gathering techniques of Cambridge Analytica, the business at the center of allegations about Russian interference in the 2016 U.S. Presidential election. Most such games and quizzes are not clear that your data will be used to target messages at you. People find the games fun, so they participate.

The Use of Data

Should data management companies cooperate with the police by handing over client data?

Should Uber, for example, share with them details of journeys that clients make? Should Google share search and browser history and metadata? If your phone contacts are backed up in a cloud server, should the owner of that server share data with the police? Yes? No? Only with a warrant?

Do you think that you have an answer to that question?

Now consider this: we did not specify that we are talking about the police in your jurisdiction. There are around 200 countries in the world, all with their own laws and police forces. Even if you consider your own local police to be brave and (overwhelmingly) honest defenders of individual freedom, are there not *other* countries where the police are instruments of brutal oppression?

Should global businesses such as Google, Facebook, Uber, and Apple cooperate with *all* governments around the world?

And if they are to cooperate with only some, how do they decide which countries are worthy of such cooperation and which are not? Is it really for a publicly traded corporation to adjudicate the question of how good your government is?

Legislation on the question of whether or not governments have the right to demand such data is in need of urgent updating almost everywhere.

In the United States, the court case that defines current law was decided in 1979 (Smith v Maryland[5]). It dealt only with the question of phone calls, and the judgment drew a distinction between metered, direct-dialed, calls, and those connected via the exchange, a distinction that has had no relevance for decades.

Trying to apply that precedent in an age of search engine metadata is absurd. In the case of the United States, the updating that is required is judicial, not statutory. There needs to be a new court case. *Smith v. Maryland* applied the "unreasonable search and seizure" prohibition in the Fourth Amendment. A new Act of Congress would need to be consistent with the Fourth Amendment, and only the judiciary can define how the Fourth Amendment applies to modern technology.

But, there are statutes to consider as well as case law. The United States, with its developed technology, 51 legislatures (50 states, plus the U.S. Congress) and its history of judicially enforced individual rights is at the forefront of several of these issues.

Let us consider the encryption dispute between Apple Inc. and the U.S. federal government.

In 2015 and 2016, this was a serious dispute. The U.S. government wanted Apple to create a new operating system—nicknamed GovtOS— that would operate in a phone's RAM and would disable certain security features. Note, the government was not asking Apple to use any existing technology to do this, but trying to get the company to create a new piece of software that would render the encryption on the company's products redundant.

This is not an issue of legal rights, constitutional protections, or warrants. For one thing, the test case at the heart of this concerned a phone that had been used by the deceased terrorist, Syed Rizwan Farook, one of the San Bernardino shooters, for which a warrant could easily have been obtained, if it had been necessary. It was not, in any case, necessary. Farook had destroyed his personal phone. This was a work phone issued

---

[5] https://oyez.org/cases/1978/78-5374 (accessed September 16, 2019).

to him by his employer, San Bernardino County. The owner of the phone was happy to have the FBI examine it, but did not know how to crack the encryption.

The government applied for, and was initially issued with, an order requiring Apple to create a so-called *back door* entry into the phone. Apple appealed the decision and, before a final resolution could be determined, the government withdrew from the case, having discovered a way to break into the phone via a third party.

The government received its preliminary order against Apple under the All Writs Act of 1789. This would tend to reinforce the contention that legislation needs to be updated, as it seems improbable that either President Washington or the First Congress gave any consideration to such issues as cell phones or search engine metadata.

Apple refused to cooperate with the government because it valued its reputation for security more than it valued its relationship with the FBI. It feared that, if it built a *back door,* the technology would then fall into other hands. If it had applied to this case only—a dead terrorist and a phone belonging to a cooperating party—that might have been different, but, once invented, the technology could have been applied in other cases too. It could have been applied:

1. By the FBI, investigating cases where it has less goodwill than with terrorism, such as use of marijuana.
2. By other arms of the U.S. federal government, such as the Immigration and Customs Enforcement (ICE).
3. By police forces in other countries, perhaps the religious police in Saudi Arabia.
4. By nongovernment actors such as al Qaeda or the mafia.

A technology developed to help the FBI combat terrorism might, at a later date, have helped terrorists.

Ultimately, the United States federal government withdrew its claim, because a third party helped the FBI decrypt the phone. The FBI was not able to uncover any relevant information from it.

This leaves Apple in a rather unfortunate situation. It maintained its reputation with customers as a zealous guardian of customer privacy, but the backdoor now exists, and because Apple did not invent it, the corporation has no control over how it can subsequently be used.

Can sharing your data with Russian troll farms change the result of an election?

Certainly, the troll farms are real, and they have influence.

On May 21st 2016, the group Heart of Texas held a protest against the *Islamization of Texas* outside the Islamic Da'wah Center in Houston. United Muslims of America organized a *Save Islamic Knowledge* counter protest at the same time and place.[6] The Heart of Texas Facebook page had encouraged people to bring firearms. There were *white power* and Texas secessionist protesters there too.

But neither Heart of Texas nor United Muslims of America is a real organization. Both Facebook pages are managed from St. Petersburg, Russia.

Only a few hundred people were involved, and if the troll farm was hoping for a mass riot, it would have been disappointed. But the incendiary messages, including the false claim that the Islamic Da'wah Center had received government funds, resonated with some.

That said, when the U.S. Congress investigated allegations of Russian interference in the 2016 election, Google testified that accounts linked to Russia had spent just 4,700 U.S. dollars advertising on Google.[7] The Clinton campaign outspent the Trump campaign by hundreds of millions, so it seems improbable that advertising on the scale described by Google can have been influential.

A meme circulating on *free to air* media such as Facebook showed Jesus and Satan arm-wrestling, with Satan declaring his desire to see Clinton elected. Such messaging does not seem well calibrated to persuade anyone otherwise inclined to support Clinton. Could it have encouraged marginal Trump voters to turn out? It seems improbable that anyone who literally believed that Clinton was a tool of the devil was a marginal voter.

---

[6] https://houstonchronicle.com/local/gray-matters/article/A-Houston-protest-organized-by-Russian-trolls-12625481.php (accessed September 18, 2019).

[7] https://nytimes.com/2017/10/09/technology/google-russian-ads.html (accessed September 18, 2019).

But, whether or not Russian interference was decisive in 2016, the potential for external actors to influence an election is certainly there. Perhaps, we should not consider the United States here, where candidates sometimes spend around a billion dollars on elections. It would probably be easier and cheaper to flood the advertising market in a smaller country. Russia takes a strong interest in its so-called *near abroad,* the states of the former Soviet Union, and is not above interfering in Ukraine, or the three Baltic states of Latvia, Lithuania, and Estonia.

Could a business similarly try to influence an election? There are certainly tools to target messages to people in precise and subtle ways. People might not realize they were being targeted with messages that related to the election. It is hard to see that any business could achieve any goal that could not be more simply implemented by making a donation to a political party: organizations that are set up to campaign in elections and have years of experience of doing it. But, such a situation is not out of the question.

Do businesses have data that could be valuable to political actors? Some certainly do. Also in 2016, the Sanders campaign placed ads on YouTube content by the outdoor activity retailer REI. The campaign had measured a correlation between people viewing that content and tendency to support the candidate. It seems possible that Field and Stream, another outdoor activity retailer, but focused more toward hunting than hiking or skiing, would have details of an audience with a different political outlook.

How Data Are Secured

Having the most ethical policy for data usage is irrelevant if the organization cannot or does not keep the data secure.

There have been horror stories from throughout the world. Some have had data hacked, others have seen it leaked, still others simply have poor security or were extremely careless.

In terms of the number of records that were compromised, the biggest data security failure, by far, remains Yahoo having more than three billion records hacked in 2013. Many of these may have been dead or duplicate accounts. This may not have been as sensitive as are some other instances.

The U.S. government had more than 250,000 embassy cables leaked and also lost a further 400,000 records from the army. *The Guardian*—one of the media partners for Wikileaks and a publisher of the cables—carried a column saying that Zimbabwean opposition leader, Morgan Tsvangirai, was in danger of facing reprisals, up to a possible capital criminal charge, as a result of those leaks.[8] The British government lost records on 25 million taxpayers, more than half the adult population. Equifax lost 143 million credit records, representing more than half of all American adults. Britain's National Health Service lost more than eight million patient records.

This is among the most personal and sensitive data that an organization can lose.

So, failure to secure personal data has real and severe costs. Your personal medical information may be released. You could be a target of identity theft.

But, the ethics of data security cannot be separated from the practical factors. Even the most genuine and comprehensive security measures might sometimes fail a determined attempt to hack.

There is little doubt that users have different priorities in terms of data usage. Some are very concerned about data privacy, and others much less so. Some people may be very relaxed about their YouTube viewing habits becoming public, but extremely concerned about their financial records.

In these circumstances, uniform regulations do not seem a productive solution, even if they are enforceable globally. Governments that still rely on laws passed in 1789 seem unlikely to keep up with a data security arms race. A better option might be independent verification and auditing of privacy policies. Trusted organizations, similar to those that certify organic or halal food standards, could certify privacy standards. Organizations could then compete on the basis of such certification.

Individuals cannot be expected to review the details of privacy policies and lack the technical knowledge to review security policies. But, a straightforward grading system such as A to E or Red-Yellow-Green, perhaps broken down into the three areas outlined at the beginning of

---

[8] https://theguardian.com/commentisfree/cifamerica/2011/jan/03/zimbabwe-morgan-tsvangirai (accessed September 18, 2019).

this chapter—gathering, usage, and security—could provide useful information to consumers.

Ethics and Artificial Intelligence

Chapter 7 (on animal welfare) and Chapter 9 (public safety) have already touched on questions relating to ethics and artificial intelligence (AI). There are two fundamental challenges: whether AI might itself gain sufficient sentience to acquire rights and how a machine might behave as an artificial moral agent (AMA)—for example, a driverless car making decisions that balance the safety of the car's occupants with those of other road users.

This seems the appropriate chapter for further exploration of these issues.

The issues are not unrelated. When Isaac Asimov began writing his *Robot* stories in the 1940s, he wanted to get away from the science fiction tropes of robot as *cute* or robot as threat. The latter trope is still common, and is the main theme of the extensive *Terminator* franchise. Instead Asimov saw robots as tools and developed the Three Laws of Robotics.[9]

The three laws are:

First Law

A robot may not injure a human being or, through inaction, allow a human being to come to harm.

Second Law

A robot must obey the orders given it by human beings except where such orders would conflict with the First Law.

Third Law

A robot must protect its own existence as long as such protection does not conflict with the First or Second Laws.

---

[9] Asimov, I. 1950. *I, Robot*. New York, NY, USA: Gnome Books.

While this certainly addresses the issue of *robot as threat,* it inscribes into law a fundamental question for the ethics of how we, as humans, treat robots. The Second Law makes robots into slaves. It overrides the Third Law. A robot can be ordered to destroy itself. The exact measure designed to constrain one problem is the one that creates another.

Joanna Bryson has argued that we should simply decide not to create AI with sufficient sentience to be accorded rights.[10] AI systems are owned. An owned, sentient being is a slave, and we should not be creating slaves.

But, is complexity of thinking processes the thing that confers *rights* as we have hitherto conceived them?

There would seem to be two fundamental differences between humans and machines, even machines with superhuman intelligence. Recall Bentham's question, which we considered in Chapter 7: "The question is not 'Can they reason?', nor, 'Can they talk?', but 'Can they suffer?'"[11]

Does it seem probable that a machine, however complex, will be capable of suffering in the way that humans and other animals can?

Secondly, there is the question of fungibility. Money is fungible. If I borrow money from you, you do not expect me to return the same bills to you. Other bills of the same value are effectively identical. People and other animals are not fungible. If I look after your pet or your child, you will absolutely expect the same one returned to you. A substitute child will not do. But, a machine? Your phone or computer probably has some practical differences, but your data can be backed up and a newer model may perform better. One AI system can be identical to another. AI is, potentially at least, completely fungible.

Theorists refer to the *singularity*—the moment when machines become more intelligent than people. But, it does not follow that we have to consider them as having human rights once that situation arises. *Freewill,* as Bryson defines it and as Asimov suggested decades earlier, would be a mistake because of the threat it would pose to humanity.

---

[10] Big Think. Joanna Bryson: why creating AI that has free will would be a huge mistake. https://youtu.be/Nefo1Mr6qoE (accessed January 17, 2020).
[11] Bentham, J. 1780 *An Introduction to the Principles of Morals and Legislation.* London: T. Payne and son.

But, if, for the moment at least, AI does not have rights of its own, it may nonetheless be acting as autonomous moral agents. Fully autonomous vehicles and weapon systems may be common within a few years. Such systems will not have free will, but will make decisions according to human-directed criteria.

Of the two, autonomous weapon systems sound more frightening, but are likely (for the present) to be limited to highly expensive missile systems. While these have the potential to be extremely destructive, they will be much less common than autonomous vehicles.

Autonomous vehicles are extremely unlikely to put humans in greater danger. Humans will be reluctant to adopt them until the safety advantages of doing so are abundantly clear. Mass adoption will only follow years of evidence that autonomous vehicles are not only safer, but much safer, than driving. After all, people who think they are better than average drivers will not shift until autonomous vehicles are demonstrably and significantly superior to the average driver. Note, this is people who *think* they are better than average, probably a much larger group than those who actually are better.

But, it is not a simple matter of adding up the numbers. Total road deaths may be reduced, but life-and-death decisions have now been delegated to machines. Decisions that were previously decentralized to billions of individuals are now being made by proprietary algorithms. Toyota, for example, has an almost 10 percent share of global automotive sales. An error or bias in the Toyota algorithm would have enormous global impacts. In principle, a system could be hacked, turning hundreds of millions of cars into weapons.

Errors might prove much less common than by individual drivers, but each error could have massively more impact.

Given the disparity discovered by Bonnefon, Shariff, and Rahwan[12] between the ethical assumptions, which people think should be programmed into other people's cars and the ones they wish to be programmed into their own, how can we determine appropriate control systems, and who should be making the decisions?

---

[12] Bonnefon, J. F., Shariff, A., and Rahwan, I. June, 2016. "The Social Dilemma of Autonomous Vehicles." *Science* 352, no. 6293, pp. 1573–1576.

Practical Exercise

Write a business case for a business of your choice to adopt a more transparent and externally audited data management policy.

Do you want to select a company that focuses principally on data management—Facebook or Google? Or, would they be likely to want to build and maintain their own trust rather than seeking external verification?

Would it be better to choose a business that principally does something else, but has a great deal of data on customers? A retailer with a loyalty card might be an example here.

Set out the business case, considering costs, trust, risks, and other relevant factors.

Academic Exercise

Write an essay on the title: *Edward Snowden should be honored not prosecuted.*

Consider arguments that tend to support the proposition and arguments that tend to refute it, and then argue a conclusion.

Resources

Philip Evans: How Data Will Transform Business, TED.com

Kalev Leetaru: Is It Too Late For Big Data Ethics?, Forbes.com

Danielle Caldwell: Confessions of a Reformed Dataphobe, Inside HigherEd

Hewlett Packard Enterprise—Moral Code: The Ethics of AI

Why creating AI that has free will would be a huge mistake | Joanna Bryson, Big Think

CHAPTER 11

Media Ethics

Some years ago, the author was teaching a class on how digital technologies change the media and predicted that there would come a time when governments would not be able to regulate the media. One student—from a large country with a record of censoring the media—immediately spoke up.

The government has to control the media, he claimed.

Why?

Because otherwise the media will report things that are not true.

I acknowledged his point. The media do, indeed, report things that are not true. And, the Internet? Well, yes, it is possible—it is not even hard—to find websites and blogs that report untrue things as well.

There were several ways in which I could have taken this discussion. Can we really rely on governments to ban the untrue things and allow the truth? Are there not occasions when government has an interest in banning truth and promoting lies?

Instead, I took a different approach: what happens if the government *cannot* control the media?

The student was hesitant. This went against his whole life experience. Eventually, he offered, "I don't know."

Then, perhaps, I suggested, we should start treating information in the media the way we treat information we get from the drunk guy at the back of the bar: skeptically. We should ask if the news sounds credible. Are others reporting the same news? Do we have any way of checking the news? Are there links to original sources?

How Should Journalism Be Regulated?

Some professions are subject to self-regulation. A panel of respected professionals rules on the conduct of the practitioner. The ruling may simply be publicized, but in some cases, can make it hard for a person to work in the profession.

Some professions are subject to statutory regulation. If journalism was such a profession, then journalists would have government-issued licenses, which could be revoked.

Are journalists the best people to make such decisions about journalistic practice? Should governments be involved?

Or, should we, as consumers, simply learn to distinguish good journalism from bad?

Who even defines who is a journalist these days, when virtually everyone carries around a video camera with them almost everywhere they go?

Science fiction writer Douglas Adams pointed out that social media are not new. Mass media are new. Most of the mass media with which we grew up did not exist a few generations ago. Radio is barely a century old. TV is younger than that. Movies—silent and black and white—were new technology a century ago.

The only thing that approximated mass communication prior to the 20th century was print. But, even print was mostly social. Newspapers were generally local, with pages of letters to the editor from local people.

We think that the technology we grew up with is normal. But, it is not. Most of our ancestors have only ever communicated socially, in small groups, and they have treated information skeptically. The ability to trust some sources and distrust others was a key part of human evolution.

Yet, somehow, a couple of generations ago, we developed the superstition that any message communicated to very large numbers of people was objectively true and did not need to be questioned. Perhaps, this tied into prior superstitions: a notion that governments and religious authorities could not be in error, for example.

Adams called the rise of social communication via digital platforms *The Great Restoration*. He predicted that future generations will ask with incredulity "you just *sat* there?" of their grandparents when learning about the entertainment and information systems of the 20th century. He could have added that, in some instances, people did not just sit there. Sports fans shout encouragement at players who cannot possibly hear them.

This was another of Adams's points. Past generations did not have a word for *interactive*, not because nothing was interactive, but because everything was. It would be like having a special word for humans who breathe oxygen.

The only people who saw Abraham Lincoln's Gettysburg Address or the first Championship at Wimbledon were physically present. If they shouted their approval—or disapproval—then the participants heard them. Being passive recipients of media reporting is an incredibly new thing.

The majority of American Presidential Inaugurations were not televised. The list of British monarchs whose coronation was televised has, at the time of writing, exactly one name on it.

Mass media are new. Social communication is as old as humanity.

So what are the principles we should apply to judging the media?

The first principle in the Society of Professional Journalists' Code of Ethics[1] is:

Seek truth and report it.

The other principles are:

Minimize harm

Act independently

and

Be accountable and transparent

There are, of course, tensions between these principles. Even if we put aside, for the moment, the active reporting of untruths, there is the question of what truth to report.

There are many things that are true, but your decision to include them in the story implies that they are relevant, which may be implying an untruth.

---

[1] https://spj.org/ethicscode.asp (accessed October 14, 2019).

A Mass Shooting

Let us imagine a mass shooting in a shopping mall in Denver. What might you include in the story? Might you mention that Colorado has lax gun laws? Is this relevant to the story?

What about the fact that Denver has much stricter gun laws and the shopping mall is a *gun-free zone*?

Would you report the race, age, or religion of the shooter?

These are all examples of things that are true, but no one expects you to report all that is true. There is a clear tension with the obligation to *minimize harm*.

For example, if the shooter is a Muslim, would you report that? You would be unlikely to mention that the suspect was Episcopalian. If the shooter was Muslim, would you contextualize the reporting with quote from the local mosque saying that this person is not representative of the Muslim community?

If the person is a survivalist or a member of the National Rifle Association (NRA), would you similarly seek contextualizing quotes?

The Aurora Shooting

After the mass shooting at a movie theater in Aurora, Colorado, in 2012, in which James Eagan Holmes murdered 12 people, ABC News briefly linked the shooting with Jim Holmes, a Tea Party activist in the same town. No other network reported that the (then) suspected shooter was involved with the Tea Party, and Jim Holmes turned out to be a different, older, man.

Some blogs subsequently reported that James Eagan Holmes was actually linked, not to the conservative Tea Party movement, but to the left-wing Occupy Wall Street group. There seems to be no evidence of this, and Holmes does not seem to have been politically motivated.

By reporting the link with the Tea Party, ABC was doing two things. First, it was reporting something that turned out not to be true. This often happens, of course. Even with detailed checking, some material turns out to be mistaken. But, by choosing to report the matter, ABC was also asserting that the matter was relevant—or, at least, that it would have been if true.

The Editors' Code published by Britain's Independent Press Standards Organization[2] sets out two clear standards on discrimination.

First journalists should avoid *prejudicial* mention of "race, colour, religion, sex, gender identity, sexual orientation or to any physical or mental illness or disability." Second, such things should only be mentioned at all if genuinely relevant to the story.

This is seeking the same balance between the SPJ's "seek truth and report it" and "minimize harm."

Act independently is another key principle.

In most developed countries, it is well established that journalists are not supposed to take bribes.

As Humbert Wolfe put it in his poem, "Epigram":[3]

You cannot hope to bribe or twist
(thank God!) the British journalist.
But, seeing what the man will do
unbribed, there's no occasion to.

Any such corrupt arrangement with a journalist is understood to be something that is shameful and to be hidden. There is no such consensus in some countries. But, where do bribes begin and end?

In general, journalists do not reject hospitality. Bloomberg, however, has had a longstanding position of refusing such hospitality. As a public relations (PR) practitioner, when lunching with a Bloomberg journalist, the journalist would always pay.

Journalists should generally decline gifts. But, some products that they might review are not suitable for loan. A motoring correspondent will drive a car and then return it, but restaurant or theater reviewer cannot return the product once reviewed.

This author's first job in PR was managing a loan pool of IT equipment for journalists to review. Computer hardware would normally be loaned to journalists, but software was normally given. In some ways,

---

[2] https://www.ipso.co.uk/editors-code-of-practice/ (accessed October 14, 2019).

[3] https://poemhunter.com/poem/epigram-british-journalist/ (accessed October 14, 2019).

however, the fact that hardware was loaned, not given, gave me more leverage rather than less. Journalists who simply did not like the product could not be induced to write favorable reviews, so there was no corruption *per se*. But journalists who liked the product could be induced to keep writing reviews. I would simply phone and ask for the product back. At that point, they would tell me they were planning another review.

The Question of Bias

Are journalists biased? Are media outlets biased? The answer, of course, is that sometimes they are. There is no way to avoid bias entirely. The real question is about systemic bias.

There is at least some difference between competitive media and non-competitive media, and this is part of the reason why concerns about bias have been heightened with the rise of digital media.

A newspaper that has a monopoly in its town or county seeks to appeal to the whole population. That makes it fairly bland, but also enables it to enforce its own concept of ethics. There is no rush to break the story before another paper gets it. (There is some pressure, of course, from other media, such as radio and TV.)

Broadcast media were, traditionally, fairly noncompetitive. Licenses were awarded by governments and covered national territories. They were strictly limited in number and came with conditions. Most countries with a pluralist polity required objective, unbiased, reporting. Other governments, of course, required broadcasters to advocate for government policy.

Each channel would have its own news show, but people would be largely indifferent between them. They would choose between channels based on the other programming and stick with the news broadcast that followed their favorite drama or game show.

But 24-hour news channels are different. There is no momentum to bring you audience from a popular soap opera. People must actively choose your channel. Bland and impartial do not cut it anymore. You want a devoted audience. The size of your audience is less important than its predictability. Advertisers do not just need to know how many are watching, but who those people are and what products they are likely to want.

So, broadcasters such as Fox News, CNN, and MSNBC offer news that is tailored to a particular audience. While much of this is about personality and style, some of it is clearly partisan. Describing the launch of Fox News, journalist Charles Krauthammer said:[4]

the genius of Rupert Murdoch and Roger Ailes was to have discovered a niche market in American broadcasting—half the American people.

Krauthammer was not alone in suspecting that the three network broadcasters in the United States brought a liberal lens to their presentation of the facts, broadly in line with *The New York Times* and *The Washington Post*, which at least had the decency to declare publicly their preference for the Democrats over the Republicans. But, whether he was right or wrong about the bias of the traditional broadcasters, he was certainly right to recognize that the old days are gone, and they are not coming back.

Journalists and consumers need to learn that this is a new world. The notion that we are agreed on the basic facts and divided only on how to interpret them is gone. Instead we must relearn the skill of examining any factual claims skeptically and critically.

It is in their ability to survive this critical examination that journalists will compete on digital platforms.

There are several new forms of competition in today's mediasphere:

- Geography has broken down. Media brands now compete internationally.
- Technology has converged. TV, radio, and print all compete directly for the same consumers via multimedia websites and apps.
- Citizens are producers as well as consumers. Bloggers, podcasters, and vloggers provide news directly.

---

[4] https://nypost.com/2009/06/10/how-fox-news-opened-america/ (accessed October 15, 2019).

Traditional media have been slow to adapt to heightened competition. But, the value of a trusted brand is not diminished by competition. It is enhanced. With thousands of different sources available, building trust with your audience is the only way to prosper.

Premium business brands—*Bloomberg, Financial Times, The Wall Street Journal*—have been earliest to recognize this. But, others are rapidly finding their feet.

For decades, Britain, with a largely national newspaper market, had more competition for customers than did their print colleagues in the United States, where newspapers were usually local. As a result, British brands such as *The Guardian* and *Daily Mail* are now among the most viewed news sources in the United States. British newspapers, just like MSNBC and Fox News, have cultivated a particular personality and a particular audience. *The Guardian* is liberal, intellectual, and caters strongly to those in the public sector. The *Mail* is conservative and writes for mothers, most of whom do not work outside the home. These are huge demographics in America, and these British newspapers have built a significant following there.

But, if pluralist countries such as the United States have faced a media revolution, the challenge in authoritarian countries has been greater still.

George Orwell's 1949 masterpiece, *1984,*[5] contains the following peculiar paragraph:

> *times 3.12.83 reporting bb dayorder doubleplusungood refs unpersons rewrite fullwise upsub antefiling*

This is a task given to the novel's protagonist, Winston Smith, to *rectify* a report in *The Times* of the preceding year. The report had made reference to a person whom The Party had executed and now considered to have never existed. Rather than edit the flattering reference to Comrade Withers—now an unperson—Smith invents a wholly unrelated story in which Big Brother praised the entirely fictional Comrade Ogilvy. Withers, a real person, is deleted from the record. Ogilvy, who never existed in

---

[5] Orwell, G. 1949. *1984*. London: Secker and Warburg.

the present, would now exist in the past "just as authentically, and upon the same evidence, as Charlemagne or Julius Caesar."

Fake news may be a new concern in pluralist societies, but it has always been a prominent feature of authoritarian societies. While some in western countries want regulations to prevent fake news, government regulations are precisely what have created fake news in many countries.

So, let us consider two instances of crashes involving prestigious high-speed rail infrastructure.

In the first instance, the government was embarrassed at the failure of its high-profile investment. The news was buried. Literally. Bulldozers were sent to bury the wreckage. The news was reported, but the government issued strict guidelines. No linkage was to be made between the crash and the high-speed rail project. Approved storylines were such things as the triumph of love over adversity by survivors. Although there are independent media in the country, most have a license only to report news, not to gather it. The government news agency gathers news, and independent media repackage it somewhat, within official guidelines.

In the second instance, social media began reporting the tragedy immediately. The mainstream media was a little slower, but soon followed. There were demands for an investigation. Pretty soon, the government promised an inquiry, with all the findings published. New investment in high-speed rail was halted until the inquiry reported.

Textbook examples, you might think, from two different textbooks. The first is the way a totalitarian government handles things. The second is a pluralist society, with free media and an accountable government.

But, these are both the same incident: the Wenzhou disaster in China in 2011. The government ordered a cover up, but the media did not comply. Even the government-owned Xinhua News Agency ignored government guidelines in its reporting. Pandora has opened the box.

China officially bans Facebook and other western social media in favor of Renren and Weibo, Chinese social media sites. But, western social media are accessible to those who know how. Certain characters cannot appear on screen in Chinese social media. If you type the characters for *Tibet independence* or *Tiananmen Square,* the words simply do not appear. But, if you insert a small spelling error, the characters appear and everyone knows what you mean.

In pluralist societies, we have to relearn the ability to be skeptical of the media. We have to learn that some news may be fake. In other countries, people have to learn that some news may be true.

Social Media Ethics

The existence of social media has posed interesting ethical challenges for mass media. Competition is sharper. This increases accountability of the media. It also increases the pressure to get stories out quickly, potentially cutting corners in doing so. Social media challenge government controls, as we saw in the opening discussion with a student and in the Wenzhou incident.

But, are there also ethical issues that are specific to social media?

Certainly, citizen journalists are unlikely to be covered by codes of conduct, such as that of the SPJ. They may not have considered the ethical issues and may lack the training to weigh up the tension between the obligation to "seek truth and report it" and the obligation to "minimize harm." The media context has shifted, and there is much more focus on the individual to consume media critically, but are the ethical issues different on Twitter than in The *New York Times*?

Plainly, people's expectations of reliability are generally lower. People will have less expectation that information will have been checked, but the general aim of seeking truth and reporting it should surely be the same.

The examples of people breaching these principles are legion. People advance crazy theories and create elaborate hoaxes. Others repeat and share these stories without checking them. There are certainly some people whose objective seems to be to *maximize* harm, with organized bullying of vulnerable people.

Do social media users *act independently?* Celebrities who endorse products are encouraged to use the *#ad* hashtag when they are being paid by the brand owner. Inevitably, this is hard to enforce.

Are they *accountable and transparent?* Despite a general sense in which social media enhance both accountability and transparency, including of the media and government officials, clicktivists themselves may be subject to neither of these things. It is fairly straightforward to set up anonymous social media accounts.

In 2010, at the height of the Gulf of Mexico oil spill, BP was subject to a very amusing parody by the Twitter account *@BPGlobalPR*. Although we learned, months later, that the comedian, Josh Simpson, was responsible the account remained anonymous through most of the crisis.

Such satirists certainly promote the accountability of business, but are not themselves accountable to anyone.

There is surely a case that the existence of social media heighten the ethical pressure on mainstream journalists. Famously, in 2004, long before the main social media platforms of today were established, a blogger exposed a CBS report on then President George W Bush as being based on a forgery. The blogger revealed the forgery within an hour, though CBS had been researching the story for weeks, and tried to stand by it for some time after the blogger's revelations. And, this was in the largest and most open media market in the world.

Adams's point that social media are the *great restoration* of social communication may lead to a generally more critical consumption of the mainstream media. But, there is no doubt that social media are themselves an ethical Wild West. The ethical principles that apply there are probably no different from other media, but there is neither a mechanism for enforcing those ethical principles, nor any pretense that such exists.

Perhaps, the greatest ethical boon of social media will be universal acceptance that ethics are not enforceable without consumers being alert and critical.

Practical Exercise

Debate the motion:
This house believes the mainstream media are biased against the government.
It is probably best to insert the name of your present head of government here.

Academic Exercise

Critically analyze one of the ethical case studies from the Society of Professional Journalists or the findings of the Independent Press Standards Organization.

You should consider the finding in the light of the relevant code of ethics—SPJ or IPSO. Consider also how the same issue might have been resolved using the other code.

Argue your opinion as to whether the case was correctly or incorrectly decided.

Resources

Ian Hislop on a free press, *Have I got News for You?*, BBC. https://youtu.be/jG-1YQ1qC8w (accessed October 14, 2019).

SPJ Ethical case studies: https://spj.org/ethicscasestudies.asp

IPSO rulings: https://ipso.co.uk/rulings-and-resolution-statements/

CHAPTER 12

Government Ethics

The Superfluous Bribe

Let us suppose you are responsible for awarding a government contract. Let us suppose, having reviewed the tenders, you conclude that Top Contracting[1] is the best company to deliver the work.

Before you announce this, however, Top Contracting approaches you and offers you a fee to give them the business.

You would seem to have a number of options.

1. Accept the fee. You are giving the contract to the best company. You have not misused the power entrusted to you. Why not take the money?
2. Politely decline. Your authority is not for sale, and you would not want anyone to think that it is.
3. Politely decline. Explain that you had already selected Top, so, although accepting the bribe would not defraud taxpayers, it would defraud Top, which was offering to pay you for something you were going to do anyway.
4. Angrily decline. How dare they assume you can be bought? You will be reporting them to the appropriate authorities.

Which seems like the right approach?

Would this be different if the team bidding for the contract was an in-house team of government employees and you were offered a fee by the labor union?

---

[1] This is a fictional company for illustrative purposes only. It has no connection with any real company, active or defunct, which may have used this name at some point.

> What if the company, or union, was paying you a fee anyway? Or, perhaps funding your election campaign and did not seek a specific promise of special treatment?

It is certainly arguable that accepting this superfluous bribe is not immoral. See, for example, the Transparency International definition of corruption from Chapter 3:

Corruption is the abuse of entrusted power for private gain. It can be classified as grand, petty, and political, depending on the amounts of money lost and the sector where it occurs.

There is private gain, but arguably, no abuse of entrusted power. You have made the right decision, so taxpayers have not lost out. The only *victim* is Top, paying a wholly unnecessary bribe. And, as Top is a corrupt company, perhaps it deserves to lose out.

But, once again, we hit the difference between morals and ethics. In most developed countries, the rules say you are not supposed to accept the fee. Arguing that you would have given Top the contract anyway is not relevant.

On a moral level, giving the contract to the wrong (in your judgment) company is wrong, whether or not you are paid. Giving the contract to the best company is the right thing to do, whether or not you are paid.

But, the rules do not allow for such subtleties.

There are good practical reasons for this, of course. If anyone who was accused of corruption simply had to claim that she or he had privately resolved to give the business to the briber anyway, then it would be impossible to convict anyone of bribery.

Also, humans are very good at rationalization. After pocketing the bribe, all the merits of Top might become suddenly apparent to you. You could convince yourself that Top submitted the best tender.

The rules, therefore, exist to prevent a conflict of interest arising. When you are awarding a contract, or otherwise conducting government policy, you should be considering the merits of the policy, not how it might benefit you or members of your family.

This is why, Senator Bob Menendez (D, NJ. See Chapter 3 for more details) was admonished by the U.S. Senate, even though prosecutors could not establish a clear *quid pro quo*. Officials have a duty to avoid both conflicts of interest and even the appearance of conflicts of interest.

In fall 2019, several different instances of apparent conflicts of interest became known, even though one of them was five years old at the time. At the time of writing, the stories are very current, and more information may emerge.

We have learned that President Donald Trump set out to get the government of Ukraine to investigate a leading political rival, former Vice President, Joe Biden. The conversation with the President of Ukraine, during which Trump had requested that President Zelensky "do us a favor" took place just days after the administration had suspended hundreds of millions of dollars of military aid to Ukraine. Although Trump denies any *quid pro quo*, there was certainly a quid and a quo.

Part of the question to ask here is not just what the President of the United States said, but what the President of Ukraine heard. Ukraine scored just 32 out of 100 on Transparency International's Corruption Perceptions Index and was 120th out of 180 countries ranked. Perhaps, in Ukraine, it is normal to expect a *quid pro quo*. The terms do not have to be stated because they are obvious. When you order food in a restaurant, no one asks if you are willing to pay for it. That can be assumed.

If the president of a corrupt country thinks you want dirt on your political opponent, perhaps he or she does not think that he or she should be limited to finding real dirt. It is clear that Trump did *not* say in his phone call to Zelensky that he wanted Ukraine to fabricate evidence against Biden. But what if Zelensky assumed that that is what he wanted? Trump did say that he wanted Zelensky to talk to Trump's personal lawyer, Rudy Giuliani, and we do not know what Giuliani said.

Of course, if we are to assume that officials in some countries are likely to interpret requests as being corrupt, even if nothing is expressly said, that does not look good for Biden either.

From 2014 until 2017, he also faced a conflict of interest. He was point man for the Obama administration's policy in Ukraine, and his son, Hunter Biden, was on the board of Burisma, a Ukrainian energy company. Biden insists that neither he nor his son ever requested anything corrupt. But, can they guarantee that no one else did so, while claiming to act on their behalf?

A lot of attention has been directed to the sacking of Ukraine's Prosecutor General. The United States and other western powers wanted him sacked, alleging that he was corrupt. But there was, in theory, an investigation into people associated with Burisma at the time. The investigation was dormant, so it is not clear Burisma benefited from the prosecutor being fired. But, it was the new prosecutor who formally wound up the investigation. This ended the prior uncertainty and eliminated any leverage his office had over Burisma. Could the new prosecutor have assumed that he was expected to do this? Might he have believed that American aid had been reinstated in this expectation?

Because, in 2016, there was an *explicit quid pro quo*. The Obama administration also suspended aid—about one billion U.S. dollars of it—as part of the demand that the prosecutor be sacked.

But, this was only one of the aims of United States policy in Ukraine. America was pursuing the, perfectly sensible, policy of encouraging restructuring of Ukraine's energy sector, to make the country less dependent on Russia. Did the Ukrainian government—or some officials within it—simply assume that, given the United States aid for the energy industry, it would be a good idea to give business to the company employing the United States Vice-President's son?

Again, it is not necessary for either Biden to have requested, or expected, any personal benefit for others to have assumed that it was required.

When a foreign dignitary makes a state visit to Washington, DC, do people conclude that it would be wise to stay at the Trump International Hotel, Washington, DC? President Trump does not have to tell anyone that this would be likely to put him in a good mood. He does not have to do anything wrong—such as let this influence policy—at all. Perhaps, he makes a point of never asking where people stay. But, if visitors think that he wants them to stay at his hotel, then they both directly pay money to his business and push up demand at the hotel, letting it charge higher prices to other customers.

Does Trump maintain a strict neutrality on such issues, drawing clear lines between his personal interests and those of the United States? The decision to host the 2020 G7 meeting at a Trump-owned resort suggests that he does not. That is another indicator to visiting presidents and prime ministers that staying at the Trump International is probably a good idea. According to *The Wall Street Journal*, Trump's reversal of his decision to hold the G-7 at his Doral resort came because Republican House Leader, Kevin McCarthy, told him the decision was impossible to defend. Many others, in both parties, had told him the decision was improper, which Trump does not seem to have accepted.[2]

Senator Ron Johnson (R, WI, ironically someone prominent in the debates about Ukraine) made a point of avoiding any possibility of conflict of interest in his own career, publicly liquidating his holdings in business and holding investments as cash.[3]

Donald Trump, by contrast, expressly did not shed his personal holdings in his family business, despite the fact it holds assets all over the world that are vulnerable to political decisions by foreign leaders. He handed day-to-day running of the company over to his children. In fairness, putting his holdings in a blind trust might have proved an inadequate protection anyway. One of the business's biggest assets is the Trump name, which it licenses around the world, and of which the president cannot easily divest himself.

---

[2] https://wsj.com/articles/conservatives-fault-pick-to-run-homeland-security-11571995800 (accessed October 28, 2019).

[3] https://ronjohnson.senate.gov/public/index.cfm/2011/6/bloomberg-senator-johnson-holds-millions-in-cash-to-avoids-conflicts-profits (accessed October 17, 2019). Reprints an article from Bloomberg that seems no longer to be available on the Bloomberg site.

The Right to Vote

Should convicted criminals be allowed to vote? In many countries, those serving in prison are not allowed to vote. In some, the disqualification can continue for many years after a prison sentence has been completed.

Anyone convicted of a serious crime has plainly exhibited some irresponsible behavior. Is it right that such a person gets to vote on issues for society as a whole? Potentially, people in prison could vote for prison sentences to be reduced.

If punishment is supposed to promote rehabilitation, shouldn't a rehabilitated person be able to become a full and active member of society? Loss of the right to vote is unlikely to be a deterrent to crime, but its restoration might be a symbol in rehabilitation.

But, democracy is designed to promote good governance. If people have proved themselves to be irresponsible and anti-social, perhaps their participation does not enhance good governance. Surely, our focus should be on what is good for our system of government, not what is good for convicted criminals?

Government is inherently based on *entrusted* power. This is a key phrase in Transparency International's definition of corruption. Government is not the only place such trust exists. Voluntary organizations also entrust power to their officers. Publicly traded companies are owned by shareholders, but day-to-day decisions are made by corporate officers. The interests of the officers will not always be the same as those of the owners. This is called the *agency problem*.

Investopedia says:[4]

The agency problem is a conflict of interest inherent in any relationship where one party is expected to act in another's best interests.

It is inherent in any such position of trust, not because most people are in a position to steer visiting presidents and prime ministers to stay at

---

[4] https://investopedia.com/terms/a/agencyproblem.asp (accessed October 18, 2019).

their hotels or because they can steer contracts to members of their family, but because there are minor conflicts of interest all the time.

Is it a good idea to hire a new person to your team? Perhaps it is an unnecessary expense, but if you are running a larger team, that enhances your prestige and positions you well for your next job. An owner-managed business would not make the hire, but a publicly traded company, a charity, or a government department manager might be able to rationalize that this is a good move.

Note here that *rationalization* is not a type of fraud. It does not mean the manager is cynically arguing for a hire that he or she thinks is against the interests of the organization. It just means that he or she is quick to see the benefits associated with the move and does not dwell as much on the costs as she might if she were spending her own money.

This is where we consider again Milton and Rose Friedman's analysis of the four ways to spend money.[5]

1. You spend your own money on yourself.	2. You spend your own money on someone else.
3. You spend someone else's money on yourself.	4. You spend someone else's money on someone else.

In the first line, when you are spending your own money, you are likely to be very careful about value for money.

In the first column, when the money is being spent on you, you are likely to be very careful about the quality of what you are buying.

But, in Quadrant 4, you are not spending your own money and the money is not being spent on you. You have no direct incentive to maximize either value for money or quality and may not have enough information to maximize quality, even assuming that you wish to do so. Virtually, all government spending, around half the economy in most developed countries, falls into Quadrant 4.

---

[5] Friedman, M. and Friedman, R. 1990. *Free to Choose: A Personal Statement*. New York, NY, USA: Mariner Books. Originally published in 1980. The 1990 version is available with video chapters.

This is not to say, of course, that no one working in government cares about value for money or the quality of the service provided. They might well. But, they may also not be in a position to make judgments about these things and may not be incentivized to do so.

Perhaps, you joined government service because you care a lot about the outcomes, but the particular service in which you work is not politically popular. All the incentives from your managers are about cost savings, not service quality.

Perhaps, the politicians who set your objectives are closely aligned with producer interests—labor unions for example. They do not care about cost savings and maybe not about service quality either, but very much about making life easy for the employees. They would actively oppose any cost savings that led to fewer jobs.

The perverse incentives of the agency problem were extensively, and humorously, analyzed by the British academic Cyril Northcote Parkinson. He first set out his famous *Parkinson's Law* in an essay in *The Economist* in 1955, and then in more detail in a book.[6]

While Parkinson is often held up as a humorist, he was also a serious historian of the navy and of bureaucracy. When his essay and book were published, he was an academic at what would become the National University of Singapore, but was, at the time, a campus of the University of Malaya.

Parkinson's Law declares that work expands to fill the time available. He also claims that bureaucrats want to multiply subordinates, not rivals.

He then sets out how an overworked civil servant, A, does not wish to split his job with the hypothetical B. Instead, he wants two subordinates, C and D, whom he will oversee. Unfortunately, overseeing them takes up at least as much of his time as did doing the tasks himself. C and D may each have only half of the responsibilities that A did, but they cannot work independently. They must constantly check with each other, and with A, so each of them is also overworked.

Ultimately, C and D also acquire subordinates, E and F and G and H. The process can continue indefinitely, and all of the people involved remain overworked.

---

[6] Parkinson, C.N. 1958. *Parkinson's Law: The Pursuit of Progress*. London, John Murray.

While Parkinson's claims of *scientific proof* and arithmetical laws to back his proposition are (deliberately) overstated for amusement value, he does cite the rapid growth of government departments at a time when their responsibilities were diminishing. For example, the Admiralty, responsible for overseeing the Royal Navy, was constantly expanding, while the Navy itself was contracting. The Colonial Office, responsible for administering the British Empire, was expanding, while the territories it oversaw were being granted independence.

Neither the agency problem nor the growth of bureaucracy are exclusive to government, but are particularly acute in this environment because of the size of government operations and the distance between the *agents* (civil servants) and the *clients* (citizens) in whose interests they are trying to make decisions.

When designing governmental structures, there is great advantage, therefore, in trying to diminish these issues. The thinking behind the design of the U.S. Constitution was set out very clearly by Alexander Hamilton, James Madison, and John Jay in *The Federalist,* now more commonly published as *The Federalist Papers.* Originally published as a series of essays under the pseudonym *Publius,* they were collected together as early as 1788.[7]

A key purpose of limiting the enumerated powers of the federal government was to keep most decision making as close to the voters as possible, reducing the distance that enhances the agency problem. One purpose of the separation of powers was to put the agency problem to the service of citizens. While individuals in one branch of government might have an interest in enhancing the powers of that branch, those in the other branches would have an interest in keeping them in check. The ambitions of one set of politicians would serve to constrain the ambitions of others.

Can these institutional barriers be overcome? Have they been?

The 21st Amendment to the U.S. Constitution (proposed and ratified in 1933) repeals the 18th Amendment (prohibition) and grants to the states the power to regulate the consumption of alcohol. As the said

---

[7] Hamilton, A., J. Madison, and J. Jay. 1788. *The Federalist: A Collection of Essays.* New York: J and A McLean.

power is, absent the 18th, not within the preserve of the Federal government anyway, this was superfluous, but the text of amendment reinforces the fact that regulating alcohol is a state matter.

Nonetheless, by 1984, the U.S. Congress had established a federal policy that people under the age of 21 should not be able to purchase alcohol. Lacking the power to require this of states, Congress voted to withhold funds for the construction of federal highways from states that set a minimum age lower than 21.

This was challenged in the case of *South Dakota v. Dole*,[8] Dole being U.S. Transportation Secretary, Elizabeth Dole. The Supreme Court found, in a 7–2 majority, that the spending power that had been granted to Congress included the power to withhold spending to achieve a goal that was otherwise outside the powers of the federal government.

Another way in which governments seek to promote ethical behavior is to guarantee freedom of information and transparency. As *The Washington* Post puts it, "Democracy Dies in Darkness." While governments necessarily hold a great deal of confidential information, which they have an obligation to keep secure, outside of this constraint, and that of national security, they should conduct as much of their business as possible in the open.

As Louis Brandeis puts it in *Harper's Weekly* in 1913, "sunlight is said to be the best of disinfectants."[9]

The right to lobby government is an important one, protected in the United States by the First Amendment. But, ethical lobbying is necessarily transparent. The Public Relations Society of America (PRSA. Full Disclosure: the author is Chair of PRSA's Global Affairs Committee) argues that it is always unethical to operate fake *grass roots* campaigns or to participate in public consultations without declaring a relevant client relationship.[10]

---

[8] https://oyez.org/cases/1986/86-260 (accessed October 18, 2019).

[9] https://sunlightfoundation.com/2009/05/26/brandeis-and-the-history-of-transparency/ (accessed October 19, 2019).

[10] https://prsa.org/about/ethics/prsa-code-of-ethics (accessed October 19, 2019).

Practical Exercise

Debate the motion:
This house believes that elected politicians should be required to sever all links with business, labor unions, and other civil society organizations on taking office.

Academic Exercise

Critique the opinion of the Court and Justice Sandra Day O'Connor's dissent in South Dakota v. Dole. Review the arguments on both sides and explain why you find one position more persuasive than the other. Some reference to *The Federalist Papers* is expected.

Resources

Milton Friedman: Four Ways to Spend Money: https://investorjunkie. com/13169/milton-friedman-ways-spend-money/
Three Minute Philosophy: John Locke: https://youtu.be/X-buzVjYQvY
Three Minute Philosophy: Montesquieu: https://youtu.be/XcKt1YgiLaI

About the Author

Quentin Langley teaches public relations, marketing and journalism at the Fashion Institute of Technology and at Fordham University, both in Manhattan. He has previously taught at business and journalism schools in the US and the UK. He is the author of Brandjack: How Your Reputation is at Risk from Brand Pirates and what to Do about it (2014) and co-author of Key Concepts in Public Relations (2009). He has worked in public relations and journalism since 1984 and been teaching since 2003. He is Chair of the Public Relations Society of America's Global Affairs Committee. He has been writing a weekly op-ed column, Common Sense, for Lake Champlain Weekly since 2005.

Index

Concise and Applied Business Books

www.ingramcontent.com/pod-product-compliance
Lightning Source LLC
Chambersburg PA
CBHW061317220326
41599CB00026B/4926